I TOOK
BOTH
ROADS

I TOOK BOTH ROADS

My Journey as a Bisexual Husband

DAVID R. MATTESON

The New Atlantian Library

THE NEW ATLANTIAN LIBRARY
is an imprint of
ABSOLUTELY AMAZING eBOOKS

Published by Whiz Bang LLC, 926 Truman Avenue, Key West, Florida 33040, USA.

I Took Both Roads copyright © 2015 by David R. Matteson. Electronic compilation / paperback edition copyright © 2015 by Whiz Bang LLC.

All rights reserved. No part of this book may be reproduced, scanned, or transmitted in any form or by any means, electronic or mechanical, including photocopying, recording, or any information storage and retrieval system, without permission in writing from the publisher. Please do not participate in or encourage piracy of copyrighted materials in violation of the author's rights. Purchase only authorized ebook editions.

This work is based on factual events. While the author has made every effort to provide accurate information at the time of publication, neither the publisher nor the author assumes any responsibility for errors, or for changes that occur after publication. Further, the publisher does not have any control over and does not assume any responsibility for author or third-party websites or their contents. How the ebook displays on a given reader is beyond the publisher's control.

For information contact
Publisher@AbsolutelyAmazingEbooks.com

ISBN-13: 978-0692591819 (New Atlantian Library, The)
ISBN-10: 0692591818

To my remarkable wife, who has shown unselfish love in ways most humans can barely comprehend.

ACKNOWLEDGEMENTS

Thanks, first, to my close friend Michael who sparked the idea, and to Judith Barrington and Tristine Rainer, each of whose books helped me understand how the modern memoir has become a new and fascinating genre.

Thanks also to those writers who clarified for me the importance of shifting from my overlearned academic writing style to that of a more personal memoir: Whitney Scott, who invited me to join Tall Grass Writing Guild; guild members who gave me very useful feedback; Paul McComas, a novelist whose fiction inspired me and whose careful attention to detail in writing became a model; and to fellow memoirist Lois Hoitengaa Roelofs.

I greatly appreciated the devotion of time and the thoughtful responses from two persons who read the complete manuscript to ensure flow and continuity: George Ochsenfeld and Edith Leet.

Finally, my deepest gratitude to my cousin Jim Hardy and my friend Beverly Feldt. Jim, formerly an English teacher, patiently guided me through the many steps of writing personally rather than academically. Bev creatively condensed the manuscript to make the story line flow more smoothly and form a more coherent whole.

I TOOK
BOTH
ROADS

TABLE OF CONTENTS

INTRODUCTION – THE ROAD NOT TAKEN
CHAPTER 1 – THE FOUNDATIONS
CHAPTER 2 – FEELING DIFFERENT IN A SMALL TOWN
CHAPTER 3 – SEEING LIFE AS MINISTRY
CHAPTER 4 – THE SHAKING OF THE FOUNDATIONS
CHAPTER 5 – EXPANDING HORIZONS
CHAPTER 6 – IN PURSUIT OF LOVE
CHAPTER 7 – LOVE INCARNATE
CHAPTER 8 – BISEXUALITY DAWNS
CHAPTER 9 – THE RURAL MIDWEST
CHAPTER 10 – SCANDINAVIA
CHAPTER 11 – BEING THE BOSS
CHAPTER 12 – CHICAGO
CHAPTER 13 – EXPLORING THE GAY COMMUNITY
CHAPTER 14 – PAUL AND NICK
CHAPTER 15 – COMING OUT TO FAMILY
CHAPTER 16 – COMING OUT BEYOND FAMILY
CHAPTER 17 – MARRYING MY WIFE AGAIN
CHAPTER 18 – A SPECIAL FRIEND AND A STRANGE FAUN
CHAPTER 19 – HOMOPHOBIA AND MEN SUPPORTING MEN
CHAPTER 20 – INDIA
CHAPTER 21 – MADLY IN LOVE
CHAPTER 22 – BOUNDARIES AND BALANCE
CHAPTER 23 – REACHING INWARD
CHAPTER 24 – INDIA LONGER AND DEEPER
CHAPTER 25 – NEW PATHS
CHAPTER 26 – BEYOND JEALOUSY
CHAPTER 27 – SEXUALITY REEXAMINED
CHAPTER 28 – YIELDING TO LIFE
CHAPTER 29 – SOUL FORCE
CHAPTER 30 – "AS GOOD AS IT GETS"
REFERENCES
ENDNOTES

INTRODUCTION

The Road Not Taken

Two roads diverged in a yellow wood
And sorry I could not travel both
And be one traveler, long I stood
And looked down one as far as I could
To where it bent in the undergrowth;

Then took the other, just as fair,
And having perhaps the better claim,
Because it was grassy and wanted wear;
Though as for that the passing there
Had worn them really about the same,

And both that morning equally lay
In leaves no steps had trodden black.
Oh, I kept the first for another day!
Yet knowing how way leads on to way,
I doubted if I should ever come back.
I shall be telling this with a sigh
Somewhere ages and ages hence;
Two roads diverged in a wood, and I –
I took the one less traveled by,
And that has made all the difference.
                                    - Robert Frost

There is no question that we all have to make important life decisions, and the choices we make have serious consequences. But the idea that we can choose only one of two options is often false.

Why is it that Frost anticipates looking back and

"telling this with a sigh"? Does he feel he made the wrong choice? Probably not, for he sees the road he chose as "having perhaps the better claim," and in the end states that the choice he made "has made all the difference." Yet he seems to feel regret—perhaps because one can't do everything. Or perhaps he regrets that he didn't do more than just "look down" the road not taken.

In my case, I chose to take both roads.

This work is a memoir, not a piece of journalism. I cannot claim that my memory is accurate in all the details. The people I mention are real (although often names and identifying information have been changed). The portrayals of the men and women in my life are based, of course, on my possibly inaccurate perceptions and my own subjective responses. They should not be taken as objective recordings of history.

My hope in writing this memoir is twofold. First, I hope those readers who are also bisexual, in particular other married men who long to have sex with men, will realize they are not alone. Perhaps my story will resonate with their longings. If so, it may encourage them to carry out some experiments to become clearer about their own erotic desires and preferences. At the very least, it may prompt them to share some fantasies with those whom they trust most deeply. Most important, I hope it may lead them into a life of deeper and more honest relationships.

But I also hope that many who are not bisexual but simply curious about the diversity of humanity will read this book. And I hope that couples who have had to cope with changes in their own identity, or in their spouse's identity, will read the book together.

Probably many of my experiences are ones you haven't had and may not wish to have. Each of us must find our own balance in seeking authentic identity, and developing intimacy grounded in integrity. My hope is that reading

David R. Matteson

my story will help you to develop a deeper understanding of, and empathy for, those whose sexual orientation is different from your own, and those who have gone through changes in their identity during the course of their married life.

CHAPTER 1
THE FOUNDATIONS

As I sat in Dr. Gordon's waiting room, I agonized over how I would start this session. I'd seen him at least three previous times. I could predict that he would start with some open-ended question such as "What do you want to talk about today?"

I could feel myself getting ever more anxious, a tenseness in the pit of my stomach and the beginnings of perspiration under my arms.

I had been referred to Dr. Gordon by one of the professors in my doctoral program at Boston University. He was concerned about my high anxiety. I thought, *Dr. Gordon will certainly witness my high anxiety today! But what will he think about my dream?*

When we were in his office, he motioned me to a cushioned armchair. He then sat down facing me in an identical chair about five feet away. "I have something important to tell you," I blurted out. It was a relief to have said it; at least it was a start.

Dr. Gordon sat somewhat straighter, alert.

"A couple of nights ago, I dreamed about you," I continued.

He responded in his usual noncommittal way: "That's interesting."

It hadn't really surprised me that I should dream about Dr. Gordon; it's not uncommon to dream of one's therapist. In previous sessions he had listened attentively as I had told about my being afraid of many of the other boys in my class during adolescence and my sense that I wasn't "one of the guys."

But what I was having trouble saying was that I woke

up from the dream having an orgasm.

It wasn't nearly this difficult to tell Melissa, I thought. She and I were used to talking about sex and about dreams. We had been married about five years by then. We were living in a garret apartment on the third floor of a lovely old home in the suburbs of Boston. Often, we had breakfast together at our kitchen table by a sunny window and shared our dreams.

Our relationship was filled with sharing—and with negotiating. We were good at both. Most of the time it was easy to talk to each other, because even when we got into material that was hard for one or both of us to handle, we knew we could count on each other to try to understand, to work it out.

When I shared this dream with Melissa, I felt she was accepting, curious, and interested. Of course, neither of us really understood the importance of this dream or its implications for our future life together. I knew it was safe to tell her, and when it's safe enough, out comes the truth. Sometimes it leaves a stain on the sheets.

Melissa didn't seem shocked or threatened by the dream. The only comment I remember her making was, "It's probably a transference dream. You should tell Dr. Gordon about it."

So here I was in Dr. Gordon's office, trying to let him know what had been happening to me: in my dream, I was aroused by a man—and that man was Dr. Gordon.

Dr. Gordon sat in silence as I painfully described my dream to him: being with him in the dream, talking to him, holding him in my arms, and having an orgasm. Silence was the *modus operandi* for Dr. Gordon. But I noticed that as I was telling the story, he was moving his chair backward slowly, cautiously, as if to put more distance between us. He continued to listen, but I could tell he was uncomfortable. And I found that inside I was distancing myself from him, as well.

I thought to myself, *Melissa was far more accepting than he is. If I have more dreams, I'll just share them with her.*

~ ~ ~

My first sexual experience with a male happened when I was twelve and visiting my grandma's tourist home in rural Pennsylvania. (Tourist homes were a rural alternative to hotels, similar to today's bed and breakfasts). My grandparents and my Aunt Lucille lived together in a large farmhouse and opened it to transients such as traveling salesmen, men temporarily in the area for construction on the railroad, and hunters during deer season. Being with Grandma and Aunt Lu was not always easy. They were strict and very religious. One of their frequent guests was the Rev. E. J. Daniels, an evangelist, who conducted a series of tent revival meetings in the valley.

I had met Chris the previous winter when our family had driven down to the farm. Chris, a boy less than a year older than I, had come with his father to go deer hunting. Deer were plentiful in this hilly, forested area. I wasn't interested in guns; in fact, they scared me. But when Chris offered to teach me how to shoot his shotgun, I was delighted to have his attention.

Chris and I got along very well, and my parents were sensitive to the fact that I did not have many friendships with other boys. So when I asked if Chris and I could spend a week that summer on the farm together, my parents and grandparents agreed and arranged it with Chris's parents.

Chris had a Huck Finn smile that turned me on, and unlike most of the guys at my school, he was willing to spend time with me. The week Chris joined me on the farm, Grandma's tourist home had every bedroom booked.

So we had to sleep on two rollaway cots on the sun porch, away from all the bedrooms. During the first afternoon, when we were working together with Grandpa in the cow barn, I was conscious that Chris's arms were already tan, even though summer had just begun. I noticed he was developing muscular arms and a broad chest. I felt both attracted and envious.

When bedtime finally came, Chris pulled off his shirt, and I could see the line of black pubic hair running clear up to his navel. I had pubic hair by then, but only around my genitals. *God, did he look manly!* When he caught me glancing at him, that Huck Finn grin brightened his square jaw.

"Let's push the cots close together," I suggested. "Then we can both listen to country music on my portable radio. If we keep it soft, the folks will never hear it."

"Neat!" he replied. I loved his impishness. And I was sure Grandma's eyes were already closed by this time.

"It's clear tonight," Chris said. "I'll bet we can bring in WWVA. That's my favorite station."

I was getting into my pajamas, but he simply stripped to his undershorts and crawled into bed. He turned his back to me and held the little portable radio in his hands – giving me an excuse to snuggle close to his bare back in order to look over his shoulder to see the radio dials. I wondered, *Will he like me pressed up against his back?* He didn't move away.

Eventually he found some good country music and rolled over onto his back. By now my eyes had adjusted to the dim light of the moon, and I lay on my side looking at his developing chest. My eyes slid down to that enticing line of black hair leading from his navel into the undershorts.

We commented to each other about one or two country songs. I rolled onto my stomach and half deliberately let my hand fall onto his belly. I left it there limply, pretending to be asleep, but felt myself become more aroused. I could tell he was not sleeping, just playing it cool. He didn't move any closer; but he didn't move away. It was hard to wait. Another song went by. Then the announcer feigned excitement as he delivered an advertisement, and I pretended that I had been awakened, rolled onto my side, and dropped my hand to Chris's genitals. I could feel the thickness of pubic hair. He was becoming aroused. That was all the response I needed; I knew he wouldn't resist now. I snuggled a bit closer and allowed my hand to fondle his genitals, until his erection was full.

I wished he would touch me as well. And as he became more and more aroused, I reached with my other hand and placed his right hand on my hard penis. He let it stay there only briefly, then moved it away gently. But I was so aroused by his responsiveness that it didn't distract me from continuing to please him. He was terribly aroused. I don't think he'd ever had sex with anyone before, and it wasn't long till he came. And I came spontaneously.

Not a word was spoken. We each rolled a bit apart. I could hear him relaxing and beginning to fall to sleep. Suddenly, I started snickering. "What's so funny?" he said. And although it was too dark to see it, I could tell by his voice that the grin was back on his handsome face. "Next Sunday's revival," I started to answer, but I was snickering too hard to finish. "I don't get it," Chris said.

But he got it when next Sunday came. In the revival tent we sat on hard metal folding chairs. I sat between Chris and Grandma. The sermon was too long, but finally we got to the prayers at the end, before the altar call. The Rev. E. J. Daniels intoned: "Every head bowed, every eye closed. Reflect on the last few days. If there is anything you feel guilty about, raise your hand." The previous year

Grandma had seen my hand go up; I had felt guilty about masturbating. She had asked me then what my sin was, and I had refused to tell her. This year, I touched Chris on the leg, and then looked at Grandma. Once again, her eyes were open. I continued to look her straight in the eyes, and just grinned silently. Chris giggled.

At the time, I interpreted my attraction to Chris as simply a sign that I was a highly sexed adolescent, especially since Chris wasn't the only guy I had sex with during the next few years. I had repeated sessions of mutual masturbation with a classmate named Phil. I didn't find these experiences troubling because of an article my mother had given. It said that it is not uncommon for adolescent boys to have sexual experiences with other boys, since they are more likely to see each other naked and are more likely to experiment with sex than their more inhibited female peers.

I found it reassuring to believe that same-sex experience was natural; it sure felt natural to me. And it was a lot less guilt-producing than sex with a girl would have been, since our Methodist church youth group was given the message that going too far sexually with girls was sinful and would have serious consequences. The impression I got was that touching a girl's breasts would inevitably lead to genital sex, and the likely result was pregnancy – and probably eternity in hell. In our home, we were taught the facts about sex and pregnancy in a positive way. But we were taught nothing about homosexuality. Thus, I never thought of homosexuality as sinful. It simply was never talked about.

~ ~ ~

My first significant long-term relationship with a girl began about two years after my experience with Chris, when I began going steady with a classmate named Barbara. Like me, she was active in the Methodist church and the Youth Fellowship. She also was a good student and had a beautiful singing voice. Barb was chubby, but she had a pretty face and a lovely smile. Unfortunately (from my point of view) our physical expression was limited to an occasional goodbye peck on the lips.

I also enjoyed Barb's parents. They loved to talk politics and were among the very few Democrats in our village. I got a kick out of debating with them. Barb and I developed a good friendship and dated throughout our freshman year.

We both dated others during our sophomore and junior years, but we got back together sometime during our senior year and went to the senior prom together. My relationship with Barb was emotionally and intellectually fulfilling, but disappointing sexually.

~ ~ ~

My first sexual experience with a girl occurred when I was about sixteen, on a family trip down to Florida to visit Dad's cousin. I hadn't realized until we arrived that Dad's cousin had a daughter just a little older than I named Tessa Marie.

After dinner the next evening, Dad suggested that we all pile into our 1952 Chevy station wagon for a drive along the bay. Mom, Dad, and my sister Lucille were in front, and Tessa Marie climbed into the back seat and slid to the center, between my little sister Carol and me.

We hadn't been driving more than ten minutes when I felt Tessa Marie cuddling up to me. Her dark curly hair fell to her shoulders and I caught the faint sweet scent of gardenias. She was wearing a summer dress that fit snugly, the white fabric contrasting with the deep tan of her shoulders and her light brown thighs.

The closeness of her body made me feel both excited and awkward. Thank goodness it was too dark for anyone to see how red my face was becoming. I was aware that her breasts were filling the top portion of her dress and wished I had the guts to place my arm around her and them. She was talkative, and I loved the gentle lilt of her southern accent. I was sweating. I was sure she could feel it, but I hoped she'd think it was just because of the hot weather.

She placed her hand gently on my leg and started rubbing my thigh. I'd never before experienced a girl touching me this way, and *sweet Jesus* it felt good. I was getting hard and trying like hell to control my breathing. I mean, my sister was on the other side of her and my parents were in the front seat! I whispered something to her. I have no idea what I said, although I'm sure it came out nervous and confused. But she just looked up at me and smiled, as if it didn't matter at all what words I came up with; she just liked being beside me.

All too soon we were back at her home. We went inside and tried to act as if nothing had happened.

Then, just before it was time to go to bed, Tessa Marie came up to me and quietly asked me to step outside with her for a moment. I assumed she was going to tell me something, but as soon as we got outside the door, she put her arms around me and planted a really hot kiss on my lips. Her eyes were closed and her lips were parted. All the feelings I had just tried to hide flooded through me, but before I could really savor what was happening we were back inside.

Did that really happen? Or did I just fantasize it? Either way, when I went off to my bedroom and was alone in bed, I gently rubbed my right hand along the outside of my own leg, pretending it was Tessa Marie who was touching me. Gradually, my hand/her hand crept over to the inside of my thigh. The caress was soft and lovely. Slowly, her hand/my hand began to fondle my penis. As it hardened, I could no longer sustain the fantasy. I began to stroke my penis myself, softly at first, then faster. After I came, I drifted off to sleep.

At breakfast the next morning, I felt some mixture of embarrassment and guilt when I first saw her. But she gave me a knowing smile, and I relaxed. It felt good finally to be getting some sexual attention from a girl.

Although I was conscious, during later adolescence, that my attraction to women was increasing, my attraction to men went underground. During early adulthood, I remained unconscious of my same-gender desires – until the dream about Dr. Gordon.

~ ~ ~

During this period I was struggling with another issue: my effort to integrate reason, science, and spirituality. Since I felt called to the ministry while in my high school years and placed high value on intellectual integrity, the conflict was painfully conscious and intense. This struggle became apparent to me at a church service I attended when I was in junior high school.

Our family arrived at the church in time for my brother Greg and me to join our junior high Sunday school class in the front pews of the sanctuary. As we walked in, I was disappointed to see that our portly, middle-aged minister was substituting for Roger, the younger teacher I liked and respected. The minister began by reminding us of last week's lesson, in which Moses brought down from the mountain the stone tablets on which the Ten Commandments were written.

"The scripture for today's lesson is Second Samuel, chapter six, beginning with verse two," he explained.

I listened carefully as he read that episode aloud. His resonant voice enunciated the "holy words" about a small wooden wagon pulled by two yoked oxen. In the wagon was a coffin-like box called the Ark of the Covenant containing the stone tablets on which the commandments were inscribed. "This Ark," Rev. Belknap proclaimed, "was considered so sacred that if anyone were to touch it, he would surely die. King David was leading a joyful procession, and two men, Uzzah and Ahio, were driving the oxen pulling the heavy Ark across rough terrain toward the tabernacle that would house it. Suddenly, an ox stumbled. Uzzah instinctively put out his hand to steady the Ark and was immediately struck dead!"

"Stuck dead!" I blurted out. "God wouldn't do that!"

The minister glared at me. "David," he said, "it's in The Book."

"I don't care," I responded, "it's not fair, and God wouldn't do that!"

At dinner that day I recounted what had happened in Sunday school and asked my parents if they thought God would kill a man for touching the Ark.

Instead of stating her opinion, my mother explored mine and then said, "Whatever happened back then, it's OK for you to think about it, and ask questions, and disagree."

For Mom the issue wasn't this particular scripture or the fact that I had challenged two authorities: the Bible and the minister. Instead, this was an educational moment, and her priority was to support my independent thinking. I can't recall Dad saying anything, but my impression was that he felt comfortable with Mom's response.

My inner sense of justice had moved beyond legalism or rules, so deeply rooted that it had far greater authority for me than did Rev. Belknap and his literal interpretation of the biblical story. I viewed God as the God of Justice and Love. This was long before I was aware of my orientation as bisexual, but my passion for justice led to my concern for the civil rights of all minorities. And my view that the center of the Christian message had to do with Love, not with the authority of the Bible, made it possible for me to be open to the many forms of love, including same-gender love.

CHAPTER 2
FEELING DIFFERENT IN A SMALL TOWN

The farm where I met Chris was a small one and could not yield enough income to support my grandparents and aunt, plus our still-growing family. Because of this, Dad looked for work elsewhere and found a job in a tool and die factory about 100 miles north. Soon my parents bought a house in the small rural mining village of Oakfield, New York.

We were different from most of the other families in the town. Our playmates were from working class families in which the parents had immigrated from Italy or Poland; most of them were Catholic.

Although my dad came from a farm and now worked in a factory, his parents were proud that the Mattesons had come to America and settled in Rhode Island in 1666.

Furthermore, my mother was college educated. In terms on income, our family was working class, but culturally, and in the eyes of the school system, we were considered upper class. People recognized that Dad was bright, although he had had only a high school education. At some point when I was in grade school, he was asked to run for mayor. (He refused.) All my siblings and I were expected to go to college.

Our house was directly across the street from the Catholic Church. Sunday morning, while Greg and I were still in bed, we would hear the two bells in the steeple forty feet away, clanging in two different tones, calling most of our neighbors to Mass. Within easy walking distance was an Italian family with twin boys, Leo and "Tubby" Corbelli, who were classmates of mine. These Italian boys and a few of their friends would pull together a game of baseball in the vacant lot nearby. They were much more athletic than either Greg or I, but Greg was more likely than I to join in and try to learn the game. I was not good at team sports and hated the competition. I knew I was different from them. I felt inferior to these boisterous, strong boys.

I was also different because, in some respects, I was a "mama's boy." I chose to work beside Mom, doing indoor tasks such as dusting the furniture or setting the table, rather than outdoor ones. Greg, however, shared Dad's interest in fixing cars and understanding mechanics. I couldn't have cared less how much horsepower was under the hood; what mattered to me was aesthetics: the sleek sculptured beauty of some automobile body designs. I remember gaping at Ford's "Futura" concept car when Dad took Greg and me to the auto show in 1955.

Perhaps not being athletic, and therefore not feeling masculine enough, was central to the negative side of my feeling different. I hated gym class. I was used to outshining the other boys in academic subjects, but in gym I was embarrassingly inferior. Dad tried to help Greg and me learn softball and spent time with us on weekends, tossing and batting a ball in our back yard. But I remained a failure at all team sports.

Greg was a year and a half older than I. I viewed him as superior in his musical talent and his ability to learn foreign languages. But more tellingly, Greg had a gang of male peers he palled around with.

By high school I found I couldn't be friends with the popular athletic guys. And Greg stuck with physically demanding pursuits, while I dropped out of them. He worked hard with my dad and grandfather to dig out an unfinished section of our cellar to create a "museum" for my collections. Meanwhile I stood around and supervised but shunned the physical labor.

I knew I was different from the boys around me, but

also there was something positive about being special. It was a puzzle for me – and I had no idea that I was bisexual, so I did not connect it with sexuality. Yet some other guys apparently did.

~ ~ ~

By the time I was in junior high school, it was clear that some of the other boys saw me as a sissy. On a fall day a few weeks after I had entered seventh grade, I found myself daydreaming in the late afternoon, missing the freedom I'd had in the summer. Finally the bell rang. I started happily walking out the side door to head for home. As I stepped outside, five or six guys from my class surrounded me and started taunting me. "Patricia, Patricia," one screamed. Several others picked up the chant, and someone else yelled "Sissy and a teacher's pet, sissy and a teacher's pet!" They moved in closer, trapping me so I could not run away. I was afraid they were going to beat me up, and I knew I hadn't a chance in a fight. Then I saw Scott walking into the circle. Scott was a handsome blond guy in my class who was an athlete and very popular.

"What's the matter with you guys?" he yelled. "Leave him alone. He hasn't done anything to hurt you!"

A couple of boys backed off from the circle, and I carefully walked through the opening, hoping no one would grab me. The guys respected Scott and allowed me to walk home, alone and shaken. My difference was a weakness, and I had to be careful. *Next time I might be really hurt – beaten to a pulp,* I thought.

Adults, girls, and other smart boys were my allies. In rare cases I could get along with someone athletic and masculine like Scott. (Years later I found out that he, like myself, had become a minister.) Mostly I learned to avoid the jocks. I made friends with the brightest kids in my class, both boys and girls. Except in gym class, it wasn't hard to do. I was successful in my studies; my teachers liked me; and I knew that I'd be safe in church-related events. So all I had to do was avoid the alleys, the sandlots and the gym as much as possible.

~ ~ ~

Two years later, when my class began our freshman year in the fall of 1952, we knew that there would be a day of hazing during which the upper-class students would tease us and pressure us to do silly things. The events at school were not threatening, so I wasn't worried about it. But what happened late one evening scared the hell out of me.

Greg and I were home, but Mom and Dad had gone out. My younger brother and sisters were already in bed. There was a rap at the front door, and when I opened it four or five of the upper-class boys were there, demanding that I come out on the porch. I was frightened and slammed the door in their faces, quickly locked it, and ran to lock the back door. But by the time I reached it, the door was already open. A couple of them grabbed me and pulled me with them toward the front yard. I was terrified; I may even have been crying. Greg came out and asked the guys to let me go. One of them, a friend of Greg's, released me. The others followed and backed off the porch. Perhaps they would not have hurt me at all; perhaps if I had gone out confidently and laughed at their being there, they would simply have teased me. But from my perspective they were threatening, and I was terrified.

For a while I felt afraid, but I soon realized that, fortunately, Oakfield was not ruled by these boys. It was a community where adults were everywhere. I knew that my English class with Mrs. Barber would be safe; in fact all the academic classes would be okay. I enjoyed singing in the high school chorus, and the music teacher, a man named Fran Zogaib, looked as athletic and dark skinned and hairy as the Italian jocks, so no one could confuse singing in the chorus with being "sissy." In fact, Leo Corbelli was in the choir. There were enough safe places at school.

After school, I had my paper route, which covered the streets nearest our home. Lots of neighbors knew my family and respected me, so I knew that the tough boys wouldn't risk threatening me near these neighbors' homes.

And there was the church. Soon I was invited to sing in the Senior Choir at church, and Mr. Reitz in the men's section was fun to be with. The other youth who came to Methodist Youth Fellowship were good kids.

At home, I knew my pets loved me. Most of all, I knew my family loved me.

And fortunately I could imagine a different future. The men in my life were not sharply divided into those who participated in team sports and those who didn't. Adult men had a variety of interests: my dad loved gardening; Uncle Hank loved fishing; Mr. Reitz loved singing. So maybe it would be okay, when I reached adulthood, to love reading and nature and being with girls.

I knew I could survive – and eventually make it to college.

~ ~ ~

As I look back, I believe I had some of the traits that seem to occur more frequently in boys who later discover they are gay or bisexual: a sense of difference that includes aversion to team sports, a preference for tasks that are either domestic or artistic, and a strong need to be alone, in part to get away from threats to a place of safety. But although I had a vague sense that these characteristics were atypical for males in our society, I had no clue that they might be predecessors to bisexuality. Instead, probably to maintain my own self-acceptance, I connected them to being a good person, a nurturing person who could help those in need.

I Took Both Roads

Mom and Dad were both understanding and sympathetic when I felt left out of my peer group. Mom was especially good at honoring my feelings. She never made me feel ashamed when I cried, whether because I was physically hurt as a child or emotionally hurt now as an adolescent. Within myself I felt quite sure that God also accepted me even though I didn't fit the norm the other guys had for being manly.

CHAPTER 3
SEEING LIFE AS MINISTRY

In early childhood I often brought home animals such as a baby bird that had fallen out of a nest and tried to nurse them back to health. In those years I expected that when I grew up I'd become a veterinarian. I later realized that a veterinarian, like any medical professional, needs lots of training in biology and must get used to blood and guts.

Considering the ministry as a vocation emerged naturally out of my early involvement in church and Sunday school activities, as well as my affinity for nurturing others, and was fairly firm by the time I entered high school. My interests in interpersonal relationships and spirituality had shifted my attention to ways of nurturing that focused on the mind and spirit, rather than the body.

The one reservation I had about becoming a minister stemmed from my love of science. I wondered if my doubts and questions would stand in the way of my being acceptable to the church. I don't remember feeling afraid that God would not approve of my curiosity; I assumed God wanted us to explore and understand his created world. But I wondered how religious authorities would react. And would parishioners be upset by my questions and doubts?

Then I got to know Rev. Beacom. A retired minister in his nineties, he had served as minister of our church before I was born. One Sunday after the service he told me, "I also love science, and I'd love to hear about the new developments that you learn about in your classes." He invited me to drop by his house any time on my way home from school. He was a good listener, and I began visiting him regularly.

One day he asked me what I knew about the theory of evolution. I fearfully blurted out the beginnings of my crisis in belief: "How can evolution be true, if the world and animals and man were supposed to be created by God?" I asked.

"Are you saying that evolution seems to be at odds with the creation story in the Bible?" he replied.

"Well, isn't it?" I asked with a bit more courage.

"Which creation story do you mean?" he responded with a twinkle in his eyes.

"The one in Genesis," I answered. *What is going on?* I wondered. *I'm sure he knows that the biblical story of creation is in Genesis.*

"Let's take a look at it," he said. He got out a Bible, the King James Version, and opened it to the beginning. "Read this to me," he requested. He listened carefully as I read Genesis 1, and started to read Genesis 2. But when I finished the fourth verse, he suddenly stopped me. "Read that last phrase again, would you?" he said.

I read it aloud: "...in the day that the Lord God made the earth and the heavens..."

"Who made them?" he asked.

"It says 'the Lord God,'" I responded, a little puzzled. Then Rev. Beacom had me go back to the beginning of Chapter 1, and count the times the word "God" appears.

"The name 'God' is there 34 times," I stated, "and I just noticed something! Where you stopped me, that's the first time it says 'the Lord God.'"

"Good!" he said, "Now you're paying attention." He then explained a possible reason for the change, pointing out that the next three chapters consistently refer to "Lord God" or just "Lord."

"The Hebrew name for God in one kingdom of the holy land was *Elohim*. The King James Bible translates that as

David R. Matteson

'God.' In the other kingdom, the name for God was *Yahweh*, which this version translates as 'Lord God.' At the time Genesis was compiled, the two kingdoms were uniting, and they took the creation stories of each kingdom and combined them into one story.

"So, as you can see, we really have two creation stories, and they don't match literally. The first starts with the lowest forms of life and works its way up to man and woman – the last living things 'God' created. But the second story starts with man, then man's wife, and only near the end of the story does 'the Lord God' create the animals."

"So what does it mean?" I asked, both amazed and fascinated.

"Well, first of all, clearly it does NOT mean we are supposed to take it word for word as history. Obviously those editors knew these were two different stories, and they allowed them both to exist, side by side. They didn't say 'only ours is true' and try to stamp out the other one. So one thing it shows is that they were trying to be tolerant of each other's ways of expressing what is holy. I suspect they realized that there is a deeper spiritual meaning in this event, which both kingdoms understood, a sense of the holy behind all the earth and its living things."

After a few discussions with this wise and caring man, I concluded that a third story of creation, Darwin's version, could acceptably stand beside the other two, and that the wonder and awe of this remarkable and beautiful creation is not limited by a particular story of how it happened.

~ ~ ~

By high school, my emotional involvement in pursuing some form of ministry had become as intense as my intellectual concern and my questions. Several adults in our church encouraged me. But even more helpful was the summer youth camp I attended. There, on Silver Lake, religion felt deeply personal – partly because the speakers and worship were geared toward my age group, but even more because we were out in God's creation. Nature had always inspired me. Gradually I learned to value being alone in nature as a path to the spiritual. I found solace in the peace and quiet of the woods, and silence became meditative for me.

Sharing my plans to be a minister didn't do much for my relationships with other boys. I remained an outsider. It took years for me to put the pain into perspective. But that pain was redemptive. It enhanced my empathy for others who are left out of mainstream society. As is often the case, what is seen at first as a curse turns out to be a blessing.

I was a sophomore in high school when the Supreme Court decided Brown vs. the Board of Education, and racial integration became a major issue in the news. Although I was not particularly close to Shirley, the only African-American in our class, I identified strongly with the concerns of oppressed minorities, perhaps because of my own struggle with feeling like an outsider and my strong need to nurture, to be a minister or healer. Justice was not simply an abstract concept to me, but a form of ministry, based on my sense of God as a loving parent.

In my senior year of high school, I became aware that the closest movie theater to us was part of a chain that was being picketed in the South because of the company's discrimination against African-Americans. Soon after, I learned that a sympathy demonstration was being held in front of our local theater. Instead of bicycling to see a movie, I bicycled to join the sympathy demonstration – my first public social action. This early attempt to help marked an important turn in my life: living out the pain of my own life in a way intended to heal the pain of others;

moving beyond empathizing with another's pain to taking some empowering action; using my wounds to become a "wounded healer" for others.

I was looking forward to going to college to prepare for a seminary education. I was interested in psychology as a major, thinking that a better understanding of how we humans think and feel would help me minister to others more effectively.

CHAPTER 4
THE SHAKING OF THE FOUNDATIONS

Mom's positive experience of moving away from home and living on campus led her to advocate for college for me and my brothers and sisters. My parents went with me to tour each campus that I considered. Alfred University offered me the largest scholarship, and it was located an hour's drive from the farm where my grandparents still lived and only a couple of hours from our home.

For me, the move from home to Alfred University was exciting. It offered a clean slate: a new peer group and a new chance for acceptance. But I never anticipated that it would be so emotionally wrenching.

Greg had left home the year before, so I had adjusted to that loss. But at college I missed having Mom around to listen to my feelings. I missed my pets, my brothers and sister, and their friends – the whole family and the sense of closeness and warmth.

Howie, my roommate, tried to be considerate of my feelings. If he came into our room and found me lying on the bed listening to Dvorak's "New World" symphony, he knew I was having another bout of homesickness. He would quietly slip out the door and visit some other student's room. I needed time alone, as had been my pattern.

Living on a campus some distance from home helped me get more perspective on my parents. When several of my college friends talked about their families, it was clear that they had not felt the level of love and acceptance that I had. I realized I had taken for granted that most children grew up confident that they were loved by their parents, forgiven for their mistakes. But few of my classmates seem to have had that experience.

I was grateful when my parents made trips to see me. Because Mom had also gone to college away from home, I felt that I had more in common with her than with Dad. At least she understood better what I was experiencing as a new college student.

~ ~ ~

I soon got to know many of the men on my floor of the dorm. Most were also freshmen; many of them were also intellectually curious and did not value athletics. Some of them even shared my interests in art and music. Marty Innet, a sophomore, lent me a number of albums by the Weavers and Pete Seeger, introducing me to folk music that took a stand on social issues. Bob Marshall lent me recordings of full operas. Life in the dorms was providing rich friendships with other young men who accepted me in a way I had rarely experienced from high school classmates. *What a relief to finally feel connected to men my age!*

Within a few weeks I discovered another place that offered both comfort and intellectual stimulation: the interdenominational Christian Association, which met in the home of its faculty advisor, Dr. Homer Wilkins, and his wife Renée. The warmth of being in a home, plus the sing-alongs to Dr. Wilkins's guitar, made these meetings an oasis in my academic life.

A fascinating and brilliant man, Dr. Wilkins had grown up in a poor family in the Appalachian Mountains, one of thirteen kids. Thanks to a teacher who took an interest in him, he applied and was admitted to Harvard University and became an atomic physicist. His mellow voice with its Kentucky twang and his lanky relaxed body exuded warmth and acceptance. When he left the conservative beliefs he'd grown up with and moved into urbane secular culture, his struggle to clarify his values and theology led him to embrace the philosophy of Albert Schweitzer, the great humanitarian physician, musician, philosopher and missionary to Africa. Schweitzer was one of my mother's heroes – another connection to the home I missed so much.

But the Christian Association, combined with an intense and well-taught course in world civilizations, challenged the assumptions of my small-town and church background. I never anticipated that moving away from home would be so earth-shaking. It seemed as if EVERYTHING had changed.

Discussions at Christian Association meetings often focused on the tension between religion and modern science, and on integrating our new learning as college students with our religious yearnings. Thus the open intellectual dialogue continued the process that I had begun under Rev. Beacom's guidance, leading me toward seeking the deeper meaning in the biblical messages as I outgrew the literal interpretations.

The discussions with male friends in the dormitory brought the cultural challenges to a personal level. Many of my new friends were Jewish. Some joined me in discussions of religion. Max Lilling was the first; later Leon Eckert, an eccentric and gifted art student, encouraged me to go to the Hillel Club.

When I thought about the debates I'd had in high school with Pearl Pearlson, a Jewish classmate, I remembered arguing that Matthew's gospel provided proof that Jesus had fulfilled the prophecies of the Hebrew Bible – evidence that Jesus really was the Messiah. *How could I have felt so sure of myself?* I realized that much of what I was taught in the Oakfield Methodist Church was not supported by historical and textual research. For example, Matthew's claim that Isaiah had predicted

Jesus's virgin birth was based on an inaccurate Greek translation of scripture. Isaiah never predicted a "virgin birth"; the Hebrew word simply meant "a young woman".

The foundations of my arguments began slipping away. It felt scary. The doubts I shared with Rev. Beacom in my high school years seemed trivial compared to the doubts I was undergoing in college.

During this period I was experiencing a deep sense of grief, a mourning of the loss of my childhood foundations. My trust in conventional beliefs had bolstered my self-confidence and made me feel special, chosen of God. In contrast, my college dormitory room seemed cold and impersonal. I woke mornings and looked beyond the bare cinderblock walls and dull brown drapes toward the sky. No longer did I feel sure that there was a personal God gazing lovingly at me.

Quietly, somewhat fearfully, I wondered, *What if there is no God?* The very possibility that my faith could be mistaken sickened me. My mind spun out possible repercussions:

If there is no God out there, I thought, *my plans to become a minister, my passion about racial equality, my longing to marry and raise kids – all of these might be without foundation.*

Fault Line
Did you ever think there might be a fault line
passing underneath your living room:
A place in which your life is lived in meeting
and in separating, wondering
and telling, unaware that just beneath
you is the unseen seam of great plates
that strain through time? And that your life,
already spilling over the brim, could be invaded,
sent off in a new direction, turned

aside by forces you were warned about
but not prepared for? Shelves could be spilled out,
the level floor set at an angle in
some seconds' shaking. You would have to take
your losses, do whatever must be done next.
When the great plates slip
and the earth shivers and the flaw is seen
to lie in what you trusted most, look not
to more solidity, to weighty slabs
of concrete poured or strength of cantilevered
beam to save the fractured order. Trust
more the tensile strands of love that bend
and stretch to hold you in the web of life
that's often torn but always healing. There's
your strength. The shifting plates, the restive earth,
your room, your precious life, they all proceed from
love, the ground on which we walk together.
                                        - Robert R. Walsh [1]

I don't remember who suggested it, but I began to read the modern Protestant theologian Paul Tillich. When I read his sermon "The Shaking of the Foundations," I immediately realized, *That is what I am experiencing!*

This crisis of belief and values was not unique to me. I now know that new peers, a new culture, or simply a powerful new experience (such as a deep awareness of suffering) can initiate a sense that the foundations are shaking. The shock waves were not from a change in the reality around me; they came from my recognition that something that I had assumed all along to be true was actually constructed from my very limited experience of life, a false generalization from my tiny sample of humanity.

As a college freshman away from home, that shaking up of my life felt like a real earthquake. When I visited my grandparents' home and walked into their living room with its big stone fireplace, seeing the familiar Sallman's "Head of Christ" on the wall was vaguely disturbing. That painting of a pale Anglo-looking man with his perfectly brushed hair seemed nothing like the kind of Savior I longed for, nor was it an authentic representation of the working class Jew I knew Jesus to have been. At the same time, the radiant peacefulness of the handsome man evoked both nostalgia and grief for my lost faith.

~ ~ ~

My decision to go to the Hillel Club was pivotal to my growth. *If I'm going to become a Christian minister*, I reasoned, *I need to understand the culture in which Jesus had grown up.*

Gradually, I felt accepted by these Jewish guys and strongly supported by Dr. Bernstein, the faculty advisor of Hillel. I couldn't possibly believe these caring friends and this supportive professor would be rejected by a loving God just because they were Jewish.

The Christian Association and Hillel Club provided a community of persons who cared about both intellectual and spiritual integrity. Worshiping weekly in an interdenominational church where the Rev. James Dick was the minister augmented my search for a personally meaningful theology. He, along with Dr. Bernstein and Dr. Wilkins, became important mentors as I moved from a believer of religion to a seeker of my own spiritual path.

~ ~ ~

Intellectual and spiritual challenges were not the only new experiences during my first year at college. There were emotional and physical ones, as well. Incoming freshmen at Alfred were required to arrive on campus a week before classes began, to participate in a series of orientation events. I met Elaine early that first week at a social mixer. I offered to take her for a nature hike as our first date.

In those days men were not allowed in the women's dormitory, but when curfew time approached, couples gathered on its front steps to kiss goodnight. Elaine and I joined them. Her deep and intense kisses were the most sexual ones I had experienced since that Florida crush on Tessa Marie. As we continued to date, Elaine was arousing me in a way I hadn't previously experienced. Yet, partly because there were so few ways to have privacy on campus, our sexual relationship seldom went beyond deep kissing.

Elaine regularly attended Christian Association meetings with me, but she was not nearly as involved as I was in the intellectual exploration of theology. I suspect she did not experience the kind of intense questioning I did, nor did she have my passionate need to integrate intellectual and religious life.

We joined the Outing Club. Groups of students would car pool to a campground or state park to attend Outing Club overnights or Christian Association weekend retreats. These events offered Elaine and me a chance to sleep side by side in our sleeping bags. Although there must have been possibilities for more intimate contact, I have no memories of anything beyond hugging Elaine in her sleeping bag, and then crawling into mine.

Living away from my family, feeling far from the religion of my childhood, I had moved quickly into my first ongoing passionate relationship, my love affair with Elaine. Elaine traveled home with me on some holidays and vacations and was impressed with my parents and with the warmth of our family. The fact that she wasn't as intellectual as I didn't seem important at first.

My relationship with Elaine quickly intensified. It was fueled by sexuality and by mutual love of the outdoors, but my loneliness fanned the flames. Not only had my family been exceptionally close, the small village in which we lived had been supportive in a way that couldn't be replicated by a town filled with transient students.

And in addition to losing my major sources of psychological support, my traditional Christian faith was collapsing. Fortunately, my mentors provided support and kept me from feeling totally isolated in my search. They encouraged religious and theological exploration. Further, I was vaguely aware that my crisis was actually the beginning of my search for a more personal and integrated spirituality, and not some tragic loss. Although scary, the process of searching was deepening the sense of meaning in my life.

During high school I had kept abreast of popular music. My favorites included the Righteous Brothers' "Unchained Melody," the Everly Brothers' "All I Have to Do Is Dream," and Pat Boone's ballads. I thought rock music and the pelvic gyrations of Elvis Presley were gross! (Perhaps the sexuality of Elvis's moves triggered a gay part of me that I needed to defend against.) So, when I found out that Elaine was wild about Elvis, I was a bit shocked. Our very different reactions to music had prompted my first recognition that Elaine and I lived in rather different worlds. Nonetheless, we continued to date throughout our freshman year.

When the academic year ended, I landed a summer job in the Oakfield canning factory and lived at home with my family. Elaine and her class of nurses began their hospital rotations. Since neither of us had a car, we saw much less of each other. Gradually, we drifted apart.

It was only after our romance had cooled off that Mom told me, "Actually I'm somewhat relieved. Elaine is a nice enough girl, but I really didn't think you two had that much in common." I'm not sure exactly what Mom meant, but the comment had the effect of bringing me to my senses. I knew my mother's perceptions were accurate. In fact, I told Mom I wished she'd given me this feedback earlier, although I'm not sure I could have taken it in. The love Elaine and I had shared had been right for each of us at the time. But now it was time to move on.

~ ~ ~

In autumn of my sophomore year, the faculty advisor of the Methodist student group phoned me in the dorm one day to ask me to lead a program for a weekend Youth Fellowship retreat. To my surprise, the youth group was located in the very town where my Dad had grown up and where my grandparents and aunt still lived.

As soon as I hung up the phone, I walked to my friend Phil's room. Phil was a Korean student and was treasurer of the Methodist student group.

"Phil, would you go with me to lead a youth retreat in a small rural church?" I asked. "It's in the same town my grandparents and aunt live in. I'm pretty sure they'll come and get us and that we can sleep overnight at their house." Phil agreed, so I phoned my grandparents.

My grandparents and aunt were staunch Baptists, but they accepted that my family was now Methodist, and they were proud that I was headed toward the ministry. They agreed to drive to the University to get us, let us stay in their home, and bring us back to the campus after the retreat.

When they arrived to pick us up on the appointed weekend, Aunt Lu was driving and Grandma was in the front passenger seat, so Phil and I climbed into the back. I was happy to see them, and as we began the trip they started chatting with Phil to get to know him. At some point, Grandma asked Phil, "How is the Korean Methodist Church different from Methodist churches here in America?"

"The interdenominational church I go to here at

college only serves grape juice for communion. But when I was back home in Korea, our Methodist church always used wine for the service."

Hearing the word "wine", Grandma suddenly switched into combat mode. She and Aunt Lu believed strongly in abstaining from alcohol. In fact, they had enrolled each of my sisters in the Women's Christian Temperance Union at birth! "How can you drink wine?" she challenged. "That's not Christian! That's sinful!"

Phil began to sweat, and I began to get angry. My Grandmother's cultural insensitivity was insulting to Phil. But rather than dealing directly with my anger, I shifted to a manipulative strategy.

"Grandma, I wanted to tell you about some of the religious services I've been attending." I explained that one of my favorite professors was Jewish, and that he was the faculty advisor to the Hillel Club.

"Since I am preparing to be a Christian minister, I thought that going to Hillel Club meetings was a good way to understand more about being Jewish, since Jesus was raised Jewish. Max, another student who goes to the meetings, invited me to go to his home for Seder.

Having set the stage for my little drama, I then asked Grandma, "Have you ever seen the way the table is set for the Passover meal that Jesus had with his disciples just before his betrayal and crucifixion?"

Of course she hadn't, so I then described the items that are set out: the unleavened bread, the horseradish, the herbs, and the four cups of wine set out in front of each person at the table.

"So, after Max's father told the story of the preparation for the flight from Egypt, he told us all to take some of the matzo (that's the unleavened bread) and eat it. I knew that this is what Jesus had done, so I ate the matzo. A little later, after they read some prayers in Hebrew, he told us to drink the first cup of wine, so I drank the wine AS JESUS HAD DONE. I think the matzo with bitter herbs came next. Mr. Lilling then told us to drink from the second cup of wine. So I drank, remembering that this is what Jesus would have done."

I continued like this, through the third and the fourth cups of wine, each time stressing that I drank them "AS JESUS HAD DONE." My drama was effective. Grandma completely forgot about Phil and Korean Methodism. In fact, for the rest of the weekend she would not speak to me. I knew as I was telling about the Seder that she was getting furious, but she didn't admit it, and I refused to stop telling the story. Anyway, about all Grandma said to me the rest of the whole weekend was, "Your breakfast is ready."

Phil and I went about our tasks with the Methodist youth and avoided discussing anything that could be controversial. Fortunately, Grandpa didn't know what had happened in the car and could engage us both in small talk. And Grandma and Aunt Lu kept their promise to take us back to campus.

A few days later, I called my grandparents from the payphone at the end of our dormitory hall. Aunt Lu answered, but I asked to talk to Grandma. She picked up the phone, and we conversed as if nothing had happened. I thanked her for getting us and bringing us back to Alfred. I didn't apologize; I just let her know I loved her and appreciated her hosting Phil and me. The whole argument was never mentioned again.

When I began my second year at the university, the Chaplain, the Rev. Dick Bredenberg, had returned from his sabbatical. I made an appointment and told him about my spiritual crisis, and the personal contact with him was helpful. He ended that conversation by giving me a homework assignment: "It's OK to continue listing the things that you doubt – things you aren't sure you still believe in. But, in addition, I want you to try to sense: if all these beliefs and opinions fall away, what is the one thing you will still hold on to? What one thing do you feel sure of, even if all the rest goes?"

My gut response was: "Love. That is the one thing I feel sure of. That is my foundation."

Another sermon by Paul Tillich became important to me. I resonated with his affirmation, "You Are Accepted." [2] Now that I was missing the immediate experience of my loving family, my longing for unconditional love was more intense.

Sometimes the only truth I could hold on to was "I will be loving," a commitment to the ethic of Love. The life of Albert Schweitzer became a living example for me. Here was a man who really studied the Bible and tried to understand it in the context of the cultures and languages in which it was written. He openly questioned whether parts of it had any relevance for our time. He pared his beliefs down to the core. And then he dared to live them out.

~ ~ ~

For the next two years at college I dated around, mostly going out with women I'd come to know in the Methodist Student group or the Christian Association. Twice in that period I developed a steady relationship with a woman, first with Gail Kelts, then with Ann Walker, but neither of these became seriously romantic or sexual.

My later relationships did not have the over-charged elements that had distorted my love affair with Elaine. No longer did I feel lonely; I felt increasingly confident of my interpersonal abilities. And I grew increasing comfortable with friendships with other men.

My sophomore year Kurt Schneider and I became roommates. He was a seeker and attended the Christian

Association and the interdenominational church services, although he came from a very conservative Missouri Synod Lutheran background. He was enrolled in a demanding engineering program, but his face and gait revealed more of his farmer background than of his intellectual life. We spent long evenings discussing our journey toward religious beliefs that were compatible with our interests in science and modern thought. We roomed together most of our last three years at the University and became very good friends.

Another engineer, Paul Culley, also regularly participated in some of our theological discussions. His lanky frame and expressionless face brought to mind Grant Wood's "American Gothic." He gave the first impression of being an introvert, but he was present both at Christian Association meetings and in our dorm room when Kurt and I discussed religion. His participation was usually a relaxed but attentive silence, but it was genuine participation, and like Kurt and me, Paul became a "seeker."

Many of the other men with whom I developed close friendships were foreign students. My curiosity about other cultures first drew me to each of them. The most important of these friends included Oli Hoskuldsson from Iceland, Hillar Ilvis from Estonia, Gerhardt Glattes from Germany, and Phil from Korea and Suhail from Nigeria (whose last names I no longer remember).

Each of my foreign friends went with me to my parents' home on weekends or holidays and experienced a hearty welcome. Since my mother had shown an interest in getting to know foreign students – she had had a deep friendship with a Japanese woman, Aiko Tashiro, during her undergraduate years – I expected her to welcome them. My dad's acceptance was more of a surprise.

On a beautiful fall weekend, Gerhardt knocked on the

door to my dormitory room and suggested, "Let's go hiking. Let's gather some wildflowers, so we can have bouquets in our rooms." I had fond memories of Grandpa, on the farm in Pennsylvania, gathering brown-eyed Susans for Grandma as we strolled back from taking the cows out to pasture along the Cowanesque River. Gerhardt and I went off together to bask in the sunshine and soak in the beauty of the wooded hills and the flowered fields. After an hour or so we came back to the dorms, each carrying an armful of wildflowers. He headed for his room, and I began arranging my flowers in the vase I'd brought from home. Right after Gerhardt left my room, there was a knock at my door. Two male classmates walked in and proceeded to lecture me.

"Dave, you are just too naive and too kind! You're going to get hurt."

"What do you mean?" I asked, puzzled.

"You can't just go wandering off alone with a guy who wants to gather flowers. Any man who is into flowers has got to be a homo. You're gonna get yourself attacked – and even if you don't, people are gonna start rumors that you're homosexual!"

At this point in my life I had no clue that I was bisexual. "He's not a homo!" I insisted. "Besides, my grandfather is a farmer and had two children, and he loves wildflowers." Self-righteously, I concluded, "You guys are just off base!"

Years later it struck me funny that they had warned me I was in danger, when in fact I was the one who was part "homo"!

Despite the fact that I spent a fair amount of time with these male friends, often one-on-one in the privacy of my dorm room, I had no awareness of being sexually attracted to any of them. I can remember showering with Oli, who was very handsome. He showed me how, in Iceland, when one jumps out of the geothermal heated pools, a man brushes all the drops of water off his skin so as not to cool too quickly in the frigid air.

These college friendships did much to heal the traumas from high school. This was the first stage of what became a lifelong pattern of close relationships with men, especially men who could share not only their thoughts, but also their feelings.

As far as I know, all of these men were straight. It was much later, long after my dream indicating my attraction to the therapist, that I realized that I had a very detailed memory of one of my undergraduate friends in the nude, a visual memory of the patterns of his body hair. In retrospect, it seems unlikely that my memory would be so clear had I not been attracted in some way. But all of these clues were hidden from me at the time.

CHAPTER 5
EXPANDING HORIZONS

After the year of rethinking my theology and politics, I spent the summer in Minnesota working with a Quaker organization, Farmers and World Affairs. My experience not only impressed me with how much gentle persuasion can accomplish, but also introduced me to a group of Christians who had already decided that inclusiveness required understanding and accepting lesbians and gays. As Chris Glaser wrote in his 1988 book *Uncommon Calling*, "As early as the 1950s Quakers were comparing homosexuality to left-handedness as something irrelevant to Christian morality and important only because of cultural prejudice."

The summer experience combined three of my favorite things: getting to know a new area and its culture and traditions, working on social change, and working with a teammate. My partner David Terrell was a warm, competent, outgoing person, and I felt very little competition between us. He was a skilled horseman and enjoyed teaching me more about riding. In many ways our time together reminded me of my weeks on the farm with Chris. However, David and I had a mission: to help farmers understand the benefits of US membership in the United Nations. This was my first relationship with an outdoor-loving cowboy of a man who was also sensitive and felt called to improve the world through teaching and social action. Working as a team with David made it easier to risk social rejection and push for the unconventional. This was also my first experience with co-leadership; I was to use this approach in my counseling and teaching throughout my professional career.

Beginning with my sophomore year, I took a paid job as a dormitory counselor, supervising other students and enforcing "quiet hours" and other housing rules. I had decided against joining a fraternity. I felt it would take time and energy away from my studies, my religious exploration, and my interest in social justice. That decision turned out to be the right one for me. As I developed more friendships and deeper ones, I became increasingly confident about my social skills and began to take leadership positions, both in the Methodist Student Movement and in the Christian Association.

As I grew in self-confidence and gradually acquired more leadership experience, I noticed social inequities on the campus. I realized that one of the fraternities explicitly excluded persons of color, and some of the fraternities also excluded Jewish men, although it was not a written policy. In this regard, Alfred University was not unique in the 1950's.

To address race relations, I tried to form a campus chapter of the NAACP (National Association for the Advancement of Colored People), at that time the best known of the civil rights groups. Soon after I had filed the necessary paperwork, I received a written notice that I should make an appointment with the Dean of Men.

Dean Bosch was a tall, sturdy, rather intimidating man who spoke loudly and sometimes sharply. Before I approached the Dean's office, I needed to rally some support. I went to Dr. Bernstein; he was emotionally supportive and emphasized that students had every right to have such an organization. He said that, as a tenured professor, he'd be sure to back me if the Dean tried to interfere.

I don't remember why I went to the Dean's office alone. Years later, when I'd become more experienced in social change, I realized that taking a few supporters and witnesses with me would have strengthened my hand. But apparently little David felt ready to deal with Goliath.

Fortunately, the meeting wasn't as scary as I had imagined. Dean Bosch asked many questions and looked both skeptical and disapproving, but he never threatened me nor suggested he would intervene in any way. Going it alone this time may have made it easier, in the future, for me to take principled stands without needing social approval.

As has happened often in my life, these events occurred in a gradual escalation that was just right for my learning about the strategies of social change. After my follow-up meeting with Dr. Bernstein I recognized that, rather than put energy into getting a new organization going, it might be more effective to work through the religious organizations that were already on campus, at least three of which showed concern for justice issues. The process of getting members of each of the organizations to work together had side benefits. The students began to learn a bit more about other religious points of view. For me personally, it clarified some of the connections among oppressions. In this case, the similarities between racial and religious prejudice and between fear of integration and anti-Semitism became more obvious.

It wasn't until my senior year at Alfred that the religious clubs' working together actually made a difference. The national fraternity Lambda Chi Alpha claimed that it could not integrate racially because its base was largely on white campuses in the South. The local chapter feared that its national office would expel them rather than allow the precedent of integration to occur. However, Lambda Chi's house at Alfred U. was situated directly on university property. The University relied on federal funding, which could be withdrawn if the University allowed discrimination. Our tactic would be to force the University itself to put the fraternity on notice: change or be evicted! All we had to do was make sure the University knew that any complicity with the fraternity's discrimination would be reported to the federal government.

It wasn't until after I'd graduated that this strategy fully played out, but Lambda Chi eventually capitulated, changed their policy, and pledged some black students.

These experiences in social action made it easier for me, when I realized I was bisexual, to take a stand as a member of a minority group. Although experiences of being vulnerable, such as my feeling bullied in adolescence, helped me to identify with others who are victimized, it took experiences of being included to empower me to action.

CHAPTER 6
IN PURSUIT OF LOVE

The summer following my junior year was a difficult one for me. I was unable to find work in my hometown and spent the summer on a boring bread route on the New Jersey coast. So it was a pleasure to return to my senior year of studies at Alfred and to my job as a dormitory counselor.

Counselors arrived the day the freshmen moved in, giving us the advantage of meeting the new women on campus before the rest of the upperclassmen. On Sunday morning, after breakfast in the dorms and before worship in the United Protestant Church, the Christian Association offered coffee, juice and donuts to entice freshmen to come to a meeting and learn what we were about. As outgoing President of the Christian Association, I made a presentation. Since Christian Association meetings had had a big impact on my developing theology and spirituality, I talked with enthusiasm about them, trying to interest freshmen in the club.

My attention became riveted on an attractive nursing student with beautiful shoulder-length brunette hair. After the talks I walked over to meet her. Melissa was wearing a white starched blouse that curved over her breasts. Small white earrings set off her dark hair and her suntanned face and arms. *She seems comfortable and very sociable,* I thought. We walked together down the hill to the church. As we sang the hymns together, I was conscious that Melissa had a pleasant singing voice. After the service, I walked her back to the women's dormitory, wishing that women and men didn't have to eat in different dorms. She commented on the beautiful trees on the campus. Perhaps we also shared a love of nature.

"Melissa," I asked, "would you enjoy walking up in the hills tomorrow?" She looked pleased, so I continued, "How about I buzz for you at about 1:30 tomorrow afternoon?"

"That would be great," she said with a big smile.

"Wear comfortable hiking shoes – I know you'll look great no matter what you wear." I was beaming, reflecting her smile.

When I picked up Melissa at her dorm the next afternoon, it was raining. She mentioned that she had been looking forward to our hike, but given the weather we decided to go to the student union for a Coke.

On our next few dates I found myself becoming more and more attracted to her. But soon after classes began I realized that Melissa was also dating a friend of mine. Of Estonian background, Hillar was far handsomer than I. He was also a wonderful person. It was clear that Melissa and I had similar values and many common interests. By mid October I was convinced that she was the woman I wanted to marry. One day Hillar, who lived in my dorm, asked to talk to me.

"Dave, I assume you know that I think Melissa is a very special woman."

"Of course. And I agree," I responded, curious about what Hillar was getting at.

Hillar continued: "But I also think you are special, Dave. And I treasure our friendship. I've been thinking about the three of us: Melissa and you and me." He paused and took a deep breath. With a sense of resignation he continued. "I think you would make a better husband for Melissa than I would."

A bit surprised, I remained quiet. I felt honored and humbled and didn't know quite what to say.

"I've made a decision. I am going to stop dating

Melissa," Hillar announced.

I was relieved that he and I would not have to compete. But also, I was touched. "Hillar, you are a remarkable friend." I reached out to hold both his shoulders, still looking him directly in the eyes, and softly said, "Thank you."

~ ~ ~

Melissa and I regularly attended the Christian Association and the Methodist Student Fellowship, as well as the Sunday church service. During October we had a Christian Association weekend retreat in beautiful Letchworth State Park. My questions about theology and the Bible intrigued Melissa but also made her a bit anxious. My doubts and my liberal thinking were new to her – yet she seemed to sense both my passion and my commitment and did not question the sincerity of my spiritual search. In fact, she began to rethink some of her own religious beliefs. The retreat discussions and some hikes along paths in the scenic canyon reinforced our sense that we shared important interests and values.

Much as I loved debates, what I really valued most was exploration. I explained to Melissa that I saw my future ministry as helping others to undergo their own spiritual searches. Melissa embraced the word ministry also. "My ministry will be to help kids to lead healthier lives," she said. We both wanted our lives to be focused on service to others.

Perhaps because we shared this common value, I sensed that Melissa didn't need me to "be a man" in the ways that most people define masculinity. The traits that fed my insecurity about being one of the guys – my openness about my feelings and my sensitivity to the feelings of others – were the very traits that made me attractive to her. Not that she didn't appreciate my being a leader. And she saw me as highly intelligent. Her love for me made me feel that my way of being a man was perhaps a better way than following traditional men's roles.

I still was ambivalent about the church. I was unsure whether I would become a parish minister or a college chaplain, but either way I felt sure that I wanted her with me. I became convinced that Melissa would be a good companion and a good minister's wife, the right soul mate for me.

I remember one particular date, a month or more into our relationship. We were saying goodnight with a long kiss on the steps of the women's dorm, as had become our pattern. The carillon bells rang the curfew hour, and Melissa walked into the dorm with the other girls who had been saying goodnight to their guys. The door closed, but I was feeling elated by our deepening love. I turned and went skipping down the sidewalk leading to the men's dorm, singing aloud a phrase from a song in "South Pacific": "I'm in love, I'm in love, I'm in love, I'm in love, I'm in love with a wonderful gal."

As we got to know each other better, we talked more about our dreams for the future. One evening I spoke about how much I loved being close to my little sister Carol and how much I wanted someday to be the father of children. I started to hug her, ready to kiss goodnight. But she held me back a bit. After a pause, she stated firmly, "Well, I need to tell you this: I never want to have children."

I stood there speechless while the curfew chimes rang. They reminded me of the midnight chimes when Cinderella's chariot turned back into a pumpkin, and all the fairy Godmother's magic lost its power. After Melissa walked into the dorm, I ran down the steps and started walking faster and faster toward the minister's home, bursting into tears.

Rev. Jim Dick had been the minister of the local

church all three years I'd been a student at Alfred. He had been part of many of the theological discussions in the Christian Association. When he greeted me at the door, he looked surprised to see me so late in the evening – and then he saw the tears rolling down my face.

"Come on in," he said. He listened empathically as I poured out my fears.

"I love Melissa, and I want her to be my wife," I said. "But I loved being with my little sister. Ever since then I've known I wanted to have kids. I don't know how I'm going to handle this. How can someone so caring about children not want to have children?"

"It sounds like she's in conflict within herself," Jim stated. He thought a minute. "She's only a freshman. You two have plenty of time to sort this out," Jim stated. He was right that there was no urgency. And I was very glad to be with someone with a bit more perspective than I possessed at the time. But he turned out to be dead wrong in his confidence that it would work itself out. Melissa and I dated for two years before getting engaged, and another year before marrying, but it took seven years of marriage before we truly faced the issue of whether to have children.

~ ~ ~

It wasn't until Christmas vacation that I got to meet Melissa's family. I was to take a bus to New York City, where her father worked, and then ride with him to their suburban home. But I went to the wrong bus station, causing hours of confusion until I finally arrived at their house much later than planned. My first meeting with her parents began with my apologies.

The next morning, as I walked downstairs from their guest bedroom, I noticed the bright sunshine falling on a colorful collection of cut glass in the staircase window. I had stopped to examine it when Melissa's mother stepped out from the kitchen to wish me good morning. I learned later that I had embarrassed Melissa's mother; I had inadvertently focused on the only area her mother had failed to dust in preparation for my coming.

That evening Melissa's mother served a fine meal featuring roasted chicken. Melissa's father made an apology for using his hands to eat chicken, and I responded, "Emily Post says it is perfectly acceptable to use your hands when eating fried chicken." Melissa's mother, already nervous about me, assumed that I was conversant with the fine points of proper etiquette. That belief made her all the more uneasy.

Despite my three *faux pas* in a row, her parents seemed to accept me. They really did not want their daughter to marry a minister, however. Their plan was for Melissa to marry a doctor.

Both of Melissa's parents were educated at a state teachers' college, and both had master's degrees before they had children. Melissa's father had shifted from high school teaching to serving as technical editor for RCA, the Radio Corporation of America. I thought this was a great job for him, with his achingly tidy thinking. Certainly RCA could provide a better salary than a public school. This, plus the fact that they had limited their family to a son and a daughter, meant that they were considerably better off financially than my family. They lived in the pleasant suburbs of New York City, while my family continued to live in the rural village in which I had grown up. I saw her parents as having higher status than mine, although I had, by then, become more sophisticated intellectually and was comfortable with some dorm friends from wealthy families.

As with most successful long-term love affairs, Melissa and I began by concentrating on all we had in common. We only gradually realized the ways in which we were different. An example was the civilization course that I had appreciated so much in my freshman year. This course combining history, culture, and the arts helped me integrate many aspects of thought. It encouraged my love for drama, the visual arts, and politics. But for Melissa this course was a drag: confusing and irrelevant. We handled this difference by my agreeing to sit in on the class lectures, take notes for Melissa, and discuss and tutor her in this material. I felt I was the superior one. (If that sounds arrogant, it's because it is!)

However, on the whole we coped with our differences by accepting them in each other. Over time, Melissa learned to co-exist with the passions this course stirred in me. And I learned to find other friends with whom to attend opera and live theatre and visit art museums.

When it came to facts and opinions, I often felt certain I was right. While Melissa was more competent regarding practical matters, I was confident about "the really important subjects," feeling that I understood issues in all their complexity more fully than she did.

Although I was sophisticated enough to present myself as pleasing and accommodating, a part of me remained confident that eventually Melissa would realize that my view was the right one. Although in many regards I am a fast learner, it has taken me many years to realize that there are alternative ways to interpret the facts, some of which may be just as valid as my own!

Melissa and I shared a love of serious music. Whenever there was a musical performance on or near campus, we were there. And whenever there was a chance to go out in nature or on a retreat, we took it. In addition, we both took our academic work seriously. In these areas of similar interests, our relationship was more egalitarian.

Melissa met Mom and Dad and my two youngest siblings a month or so after we began dating. My parents immediately liked her, and she found them both very warm. She especially appreciated my dad's affection.

On later visits home Melissa met my sister Lucille and her boyfriend; they both were attending a state teacher's college in the northeastern part of the state, and their relationship, like ours, was becoming serious. So some of our visits to my parents' home felt like double dating.

I think the acceptance Melissa felt from my parents increased her trust that my love for her was genuine and rooted in a more healthy family experience than the one in which she had grown up. This may have helped her feel comfortable with our increasing sexual intimacy.

That intimacy deepened on one of the trips Melissa took with me to my parents' home. Dad was working and Mom had shopping to do, so Melissa and I were alone in the house. When we finished cleaning up the breakfast table and doing the dishes, I suggested, "Let's go up to my bedroom."

In the "boys' bedroom" there were still three single beds for Greg, Len and me. Perhaps we took a nap first, but at some point Melissa said: "I need to practice a nursing technique. Let me give you a bed bath."

First, she gathered a container of warm water, washcloths, a bar of soap, and some towels. "I want you to just lie here, as if you're a sick patient," she told me. She then proceeded to undress me – a process that I found very arousing. Gently and caringly Melissa washed me from head to toe, every part of my body. Noticing my erection, Melissa moved beyond the usual procedures of nursing care, tenderly and lovingly giving me a genital massage.

In the mid-fifties, most committed Protestant Christians still held that sexual intercourse should be delayed until marriage. But many in our age group felt that, short of intercourse and in the context of a loving relationship, sexual intimacy including genital contact was permissible. It was helpful that Melissa and I had a similar background regarding interpersonal ethics. We trusted each other to care about more than our own selfish pleasure. Caring was the central value for each of us. I had personally reached the conclusion that if a couple had made a clear commitment to each other, even intercourse was permissible before marriage. But Melissa did not share this view. Even after we became engaged, Melissa and I had different views of what was sexually permissible between us, and I respected her wishes.

Except in that early adolescent experience with Chris and with one other boy, I had not previously reached orgasm with another person until it became part of lovemaking for Melissa and me. The experience of bringing the other to orgasm felt deeply gratifying and intensely intimate for both of us, and delaying full intercourse until marriage did not foster any resentment. At that time, we did not expect to marry until Melissa had graduated from college, well over two years away.

I think there is something wonderful about being inexperienced in lovemaking, experimenting together as we learned about our own and each other's bodies. I don't subscribe to the idea that a couple should enter into a relationship with advanced sexual skills and expect everything to go smoothly. That view seems to me a misappropriation of a technical and mechanical perspective to a highly individual and personal experience. Learning to really listen to each other – and to give accurate feedback on what each of us wanted, and what pleased or didn't please each of us – was an important benefit of our inexperience. If the central meaning of prayer is to listen carefully without predetermined outcomes, then I feel that our physical exploration was a form of prayer.

~ ~ ~

More than a year had passed since I had begun dating Melissa. I had completed my B.A. and was attending seminary, while Melissa was continuing her undergraduate work at medical centers affiliated with Alfred U. Although I realized that choosing whom to marry was one of the most important decisions of my life, it was clear to me I'd chosen Melissa. The only area I thought might cause conflict was the issue of children.

I began to understand why Melissa didn't want to be a mother. Once, when I commented about how hard she worked, Melissa explained, "I guess it's a habit. I've had to do most of the housework since I was a kid. My mother never felt up to it. She was sick a lot."

As I learned more about her childhood, I came to believe that Melissa's reluctance to have children emerged from negative experiences in her own family life and her fear that she could not be an adequate mother. I suspected that when she realized that my love for her was trustworthy and as she became more and more a part of my loving family, she would see that she could do a good job of raising children. That hunch played a part in my decision to propose to her.

It was a sunny Saturday, March 10, 1961, a week before the student dance at the seminary on St. Patrick's Day, when my roommate Ray went with me to pick out an engagement ring for Melissa.

After the dance the next weekend, we went back to my seminary dorm room. I gave her the package with the engagement ring, and as she opened it I asked her to marry me. It took her by surprise. She was only a sophomore, and her parents insisted that she shouldn't even think of marriage until she had completed her bachelor's degree. But by this time she knew she wanted to marry me, so without hesitation she said "Yes."

~ ~ ~

David R. Matteson

In the spring of my senior year at college, I needed to make a decision about where I would continue my education. Melissa would remain in her BS/RN nursing program at hospitals in Western New York and Pennsylvania for the next two years. What made the most sense was for me to enroll at Colgate Rochester Divinity School (CRDS), only a few hours' drive from where Melissa would be, so she and I could see each other some weekends. The Rev. James Dick, the minister of the university church, had studied at that seminary. My reservations about it at the time concerned its emphasis on Neo-Orthodox theology. But I didn't think I could stand being as far away as Massachusetts, North Carolina, or Colorado, where the more liberal Methodist schools were located.

Should I attend a school where I don't really agree with their theology in order to stay close to the woman I love? was the way I thought about the issue at first. As usual, I tried to resolve this question by gathering more data, not so much cognitive information as face-to-face experience. I went to Colgate Rochester to talk with both students and professors. I found that the seminary strongly encouraged exploration and soul-searching; the issue shifted from "What theology characterizes the school?" to "What is the climate for personal and spiritual growth?" Although as a liberal I might be in a minority at CRDS, the setting seemed a good one for continuing my exploration, for pursuing my unique spiritual path. Colgate Rochester fostered a stimulating intellectual environment and included students of many denominations. I already doubted that I would remain Methodist, and attending a school outside that tradition might help me choose what denomination I would move into.

Melissa and I continued to see each other regularly. By

spring of my senior year of seminary, we were planning how to spend many weekends together. Sometimes Melissa would come to Rochester and stay in the small women's dorm at CRDS; sometimes I would camp out near one of her hospital placements; and most frequently she would find a ride to Oakfield, where we could reunite at my parents' home. We were both ready for a new phase in our lives.

CHAPTER 7
LOVE INCARNATE

It's hard to know how much my longing to stay close to Melissa influenced my perception of CRDS, but I made the right decision. CRDS provided the richest experiential education, the deepest emotional ties, and the most creative teaching of any institution of higher education I have ever attended

My roommate Ray Wells and I developed a strong and safe friendship. Ray was a wonderfully gentle person. He understood that I needed encouragement to accept my body, and I understood that he needed tutoring and dialogue in understanding theology.

Ray and I often used the bowling alley in the basement of our dorm, since bowling was one of the few physical exercises I enjoyed. But with Ray's help, I began to explore other activities and to feel more self-esteem. The two years Ray and I lived together provided a rich experience in a fully mutual male-male relationship with almost no tension or competition. Ray sometimes felt inferior to me intellectually, and I was sometimes too assertive socially, causing him to feel left out. But these were concerns we could talk about. In physical matters, he was my mentor, and I deeply appreciated that.

We felt no sexual tension, and it's hard to know quite why. Perhaps it was because I was still unaware of my bisexuality, and because Ray was clearly heterosexual. Although Ray and I were comfortable changing in front of each other, I do not have memories of him that were sexualized. I always remember his soft and warm smile. I think he took life a bit more lightly than I did in those years.

By the end of our first year together, Ray, a female classmate named Joni, and I had become like a set of triplets. Our deeply affectionate brother-brother-sister relationship replicated the one I had had with my siblings Greg and Lucille. Ray, Joni and I spent lots of time studying together, but we also hiked in state parks, went on picnics, and drove to Lake Ontario.

Melissa grew to trust that my relationship with Joni was not a threat. Already Melissa and I had developed consistently honest communication, which helped her to transcend jealousy concerning my other deep relationships. This became crucial to our later dealings with my bisexuality.

In 1962, my third year in the seminary, I was elected president of the student body. This was the closest thing to being popular among my peers that I had ever experienced. I was finally with a group that shared my values, and I felt a deep sense of belonging. As student body president, I officially represented (and fought for) the students' views on issues, which brought me into public conflict with the president of the seminary, Dr. Gene Bartlett. We both handled our disagreements with respect for each other's personal integrity.

My experience at CRDS also helped me move beyond intellectualizing to become more aware of my own bodily and emotional experience. I understood that my ability to minister, regardless of what form it took, would require me to know my own emotions.

~ ~ ~

Following my first year of seminary, I interviewed for a summer job in a center for emotionally disturbed six- to twelve-year-olds. The director Dr. Koret, a short man with a broad smile, put me at ease with his warmth and personal interest in me. He struck me as brilliant as well as kind. After our interview, Dr. Koret encouraged me to eat lunch in one of the cottages where the children lived, to get a feel for the job.

The spacious campus had three cottages, each housing eight children. I walked into one of these cottages and sat down with staff and kids at one of the two dining tables, with my back to a window. The dining room was a few feet below ground level, so the windowsill behind me was just above my shoulder, but outside the window was less than a foot above the sloping ground.

While talking with the staff member at my table, I noticed the children had begun to giggle. Suddenly I felt warm liquid pouring on my shoulder. I jerked around, and saw a boy standing outside the open window, pissing on me! This was my introduction to Frankie. There was no question that this would be a challenging job, but I took it.

The first day I came to work I saw Frankie playing in the swimming pool. I joined the kids in the water. Frankie splashed me in a friendly way and then asked to get on my shoulders. For some reason, he focused on me constantly. Within a week, I seemed to have become a sort of father or big brother to him – and the target for his aggression.

Normally I worked in the afternoon, but one day when the Center was short-staffed, I was asked to stay over to work the evening shift as well. After we had put the kids in our cottage to bed, the other staff member went home, and I was left alone with the children.

Soon all was quiet. I assumed all the kids were asleep, and I settled down at one of the dining room tables, my back to the steps leading up to the bedrooms, and began working on an assignment for one of my classes.

I had been concentrating on my homework for about an hour when I suddenly heard running water behind me. I jumped up and saw a small river running down the corridor from the kids' bedrooms and streaming down the steps into the dining room. I rushed upstairs into the bathrooms and discovered that all the sinks had been stopped up, the toilet bowls were stuffed with towels, and every faucet was running full blast! As I turned off all the water, the kids were laughing and running outdoors. Soon they had awakened all 24 kids in the three cottages.

With only the two night staffers from the other cottages and me, it took an hour to round up all the children and settle them back in their beds. But finally, all was quiet again, and I resumed my homework.

Almost as soon as I had re-opened my textbook, I heard water running again. *Holy Shit!* The whole episode was repeating itself! This time it was clear to me that Frankie was the instigator.

When everyone was settled down again, even Frankie, I opened my books to do my homework. And again I heard the sound of running water. The whole scene occurred for still a third time!

By then I was furious. I caught Frankie, carried him straight to his room, picked him up, and hurled him across the room toward his bed.

My God! I thought to myself as I watched him flying across the room. *He could smash against the cinderblock wall behind his bed!* Fortunately he landed right on the bed, unhurt.

I don't know which of us was more appalled by my anger and this reckless act. I do know an inner voice told me, *You could have seriously injured this kid*. After my heart stopped racing, I said to myself, *I have no right to be working here. I can't believe I could get so riled up. I'm a minister, not a violent man.*

At 9:00 the next morning I phoned Dr. Koret's office and asked for the earliest possible appointment with the director. A few hours later I walked into his office. Dr. Koret greeted me with his usual warmth.

"I'm here to resign," I informed him. "I don't belong

here." I explained last night's scene and my irresponsible behavior.

Dr. Koret was an exceptionally good listener. When I had finished, he said calmly, "I'm not going to accept your resignation. You are the kind of person we need here. It's clear you care about these kids. And don't think you are the first staff member to respond in anger. Usually I hear about such treatment of the kids secondhand. I appreciate your coming directly to me about this."

His keeping me on the staff touched me. More important, I felt forgiven. Once again in my experience, a Jewish person was offering me the experience of grace that I'd been taught came only through Christ. The event revealed to me a piece of myself I had not previously acknowledged: I, too, can become an angry and vindictive person. I continue to be thankful to Frankie for forcing me to recognize a part of me, which, before this encounter, had been relegated to my "shadow."

Not only did my work under Dr. Koret increase my awareness of my own emotions; it also deepened my respect for inclusiveness. I was learning to be more Christ-like from a Jew! Although at this time I still had no awareness of my bisexuality, I knew that inclusiveness was a key to true democracy and to genuine spiritual community

~ ~ ~

Back at seminary, Ray and I had field assignments working primarily with high school students in churches of our own denominations, his Baptist, mine Methodist. So Sundays were busy days.

I was studying in my dorm one Monday in late May when another student knocked and said, "Dave, there's a phone call for you." When I walked to the other end of the dormitory hall and picked up the receiver, I recognized the voice of the D.S., the District Superintendent of the

Rochester conference of the Methodist Church. I was surprised. My ambivalent feelings about the Methodist denomination flashed through my mind.

"Hi,. I know you've been doing a good job this year working as a youth minister in the Culver Avenue church here in Rochester. There's an opportunity for you to have a more responsible position, and I think you're ready for it. Is that something you're willing to consider?"

A few days later, we met in his office to discuss my becoming part-time minister of a small church in a village only thirty minutes from the seminary. "There is no parsonage," the D.S. told me. "You can continue to live on the seminary campus. You'd need to go out to Churchville once a week to call on your parishioners and to attend some committee meetings. And of course you'd lead the service and preach on Sundays, too."

Since Churchville was a rural town similar to the one in which I'd grown up, this pastorate sounded like a good fit and a valuable experience. I agreed to take the position starting in the summer of 1961, knowing it would give me concrete experience with the Methodist system, which might help me decide whether to be ordained Methodist or to leave the denomination.

Soon after arriving, I offered the parishioners a new service: pastoral counseling, an area of ministry in which I felt especially well trained. Months later two laymen, both about my age, approached me about starting a men's Bible study group. I was excited about the chance to teach something I was learning about in seminary, the history of the writing and compilation of the Bible. I gladly agreed to lead the group. This was my first experience with the power of small committed groups in the church and my first awareness of the value of groups limited to one gender.

The men in this small group began sharing their

questions and doubts, as well as their intellectual curiosity about the Bible. Gradually they developed a level of trust and sharing that is rare between men in most settings, showing me how healing male-to-male intimacy can be. This and other pastoral and educational efforts helped me get to know a few members, including some of this church's key leaders.

Unfortunately, I did not connect so well with those who regularly attended church but weren't interested in study groups or counseling. My sermons tended to be too intellectual for many members who had, at most, high school educations. Toward the end of the church year, the D.S. called me into his office.

"I want you to know, David, that a group of lay people came to see me to discuss your ministry. They're dissatisfied with your style. They've asked me not to re-appoint you."

I was devastated. *Why hadn't they told me directly if they weren't happy with me?*

The D.S. read my expression. "I am going to re-appoint you to the church. But I want you to know about this, so you can think about how you can minister better to these people."

I appreciated his giving me this feedback. And I was grateful that I had a supportive situation at the seminary, away from the stresses of the ministry, in which to heal my wounds and learn from my mistakes. This experience helped me to become clearer about my own strengths and weaknesses, and to determine the form my future ministry would take.

It also clarified what I believed was a serious flaw in the Methodist system of that time. The structure made it easy for parishioners who have criticisms of their minister to complain to the superintendent rather than give the minister direct feedback. It might have been healthier if the D.S. had offered to mediate and urged the parishioners involved to talk to me directly in a meeting that he would moderate. That might have opened up communication between us. I began to observe the dynamics and structure of social systems, not just individuals. That led to my specializing in family and couple therapies, and continuing to engage in social activism to change the larger systems.

In spite of this painful experience, the work with the Churchville congregation had some very positive outcomes. Two or three men who had been in the Bible Study Group approached me months after the group disbanded and expressed their concern regarding race relations in the area. These men had the foresight to realize – given that the church was in the exurbs of Rochester, a city with both economic problems and racial tensions – that African-Americans might soon begin moving into their community. They wondered if there was some way we could help the community prepare.

Together we decided that any effort would be more effective if it involved all three of the churches in the village. We were able to persuade the priest or minister and two laymen from each to meet regularly to think through this potential challenge.

After a few meetings of these nine delegates, a member of the group pointed out, "Here we are, a totally white group, discussing black/white race relations." Another member noted, "There is a Negro Baptist church only ten miles from here." The group decided to contact that church and ask them to choose some people to join our discussion. They agreed, and we all looked forward to the next meeting, expecting that the Baptist minister and a couple of laypersons would join us.

On the evening of the next meeting, car after car of African-American Baptists arrived and filed into our church! Much to our surprise, the meeting consisted of roughly thirty-five blacks joining nine whites. Somehow they had thought that their whole congregation was invited.

We all laughed at the misunderstanding, but it was a memorable experience for many of the white church members and clergy. For most of us, this was the first time in our lives we'd been in the minority in a mixed racial situation. The committee was off to a good start.

This experience in inclusiveness and the unexpected lesson in empathy reaffirmed my commitment to a ministry and family life dedicated to breaking down barriers.

~ ~ ~

During the years that I was serving as pastor, parishioners in my small church were very supportive of my relationship with Melissa. By that time Melissa and I were well into our second year of a commuter relationship. We both wanted to marry without waiting for Melissa to finish her B.S. and R.N. Although Melissa's parents had wanted her to finish her undergraduate work before marriage, when we were engaged and planning to marry in the summer after Melissa had competed her junior year, they were supportive. They even generously offered to continue to pay Melissa's tuition for her final year of college.

Melissa's father had once considered the ministry and was fascinated by biblical research and criticism. He had a tendency to glue himself to me when we visited. At the time, I found this annoying; I needed some personal space to unwind from the tension of living in the world of intellectualism and order. Now I regret that I was not more receptive to his attachment to me.

Melissa and I both loved the beautiful Tudor chapel at the seminary, as well as its excellent pipe organ. The decision to hold our wedding and reception at the seminary, rather than near Melissa's parents' home, made it easier for my family, the members of my church, and our college and seminary friends to attend. It also meant all the planning was up to us.

Surprisingly, the only hurdle we had as a result of choosing the seminary chapel was that Melissa and I were planning to have dancing at our wedding reception. Until our request, the school had never had to make a formal decision about this issue. They approved, so our wedding was the first one on campus to include dancing. Since both Melissa and I wanted my brother Greg to play the organ at our wedding, I chose Ray to be my best man. (My friendship with Ray continued right up until his premature death in 2007. Ray eventually left parish ministry and became a flight instructor for pilots of small planes. He also forecasted the weather for a radio station in North Carolina, where his daily reports included some homespun philosophy. The philosophy parts, he explained to me, were his sermons.)

Although the organ music, the Tudor architecture of the seminary chapel, and the bright sunny day all contributed to a beautiful wedding, it was the presence of almost all of our closest friends and our families that made it truly a community of souls witnessing our commitment. Both Melissa and I wanted to make every element of the service fit our values, our tastes and our beliefs. We chose each piece of music. We wrote each part of the ceremony, making sure the words fit our own feelings and beliefs.

We were not the first to do this. The seminary was a culture of seekers who often reworked tradition to shape it into an authentic personal statement. Our vows were more powerful because they expressed exactly what we felt and believed at that time. Of course, neither of us had any clue of what I would discover later: my own bisexuality.

So this, the second of the three biggest decisions of my

life, seemed completely right to me. I know that often men and women have qualms as the wedding date approaches, but I fully enjoyed planning the wedding with Melissa and longed for the culmination of our love and the closeness of living together each day.

The wedding went beautifully in every detail. We both felt very much supported by our parents, our siblings, and the wedding party consisting of some of our closest friends. The words we spoke fit us so personally that on each anniversary for many years we re-read the service to each other.

Our anticipation of full sexual union was intense. We had talked to two of my seminary professors about birth control and how important it was to delay having children until we both had competed our graduate degrees. Soon after the service and reception we headed off to the Rideau Lakes in Ontario Canada. Just as we were entering Canada, Melissa gasped. "I just realized, I never packed the diaphragm!"

"It's Okay, hon," I assured her. "I'm sure we can get one in a pharmacy in Canada." We found a drug store in the next village, and I walked in and asked to purchase a diaphragm. The pharmacist looked puzzled and asked, "*Parlez-vous français?*" He didn't understand English. Although I had taken French in both high school and college, "diaphragm" was not part of the required vocabulary. I thought a moment, and then formed a circle with my thumb and forefinger. The pharmacist shrugged his shoulders and continued to look puzzled.

I pointed to my new wedding ring, then pointed to my groin, and made the circle again with my hand, and started to laugh.

"*O, mais oui!*" the pharmacist said, laughing with me – and he got out some condoms as well as several diaphragms. Problem solved.

~ ~ ~

For most of our married lives, our sexual relationship has been very satisfying and frequently a window into the transcendent. Certainly there have been times of disappointment, but I don't remember ever having an argument about the process of our lovemaking. There were times I wished for more frequent sex than Melissa wanted. And there were times in the 1970s when my emerging bisexual awareness and Melissa's reactions got in the way, resulting in transitory periods of erectile dysfunction. In almost all areas of life Melissa has been incredibly tolerant when things haven't gone as planned or expected. For both of us, the sense of closeness and love has been far more important than whether specific sexual events had a Hollywood ending. Although I believe that sexuality is a holy gift and an important one, neither of us confuses sexual performance with love.

~ ~ ~

In the late 1950s and into the 1960s, men's and women's roles were stereotyped, and in many ways the job assignments Melissa and I had within our relationship reflected that. Even before we were married, Melissa did most of my ironing. I had a car soon after I started seminary, and I did all the driving at first because Melissa did not know how to drive. When she got a learner's permit, I was her driving instructor – a good way to test communications!

In the home in which I grew up, we three older siblings washed and dried the dishes and put them in the cupboard. So Melissa and I shared these tasks. But cooking was entirely her responsibility. I was so inept as a cook that Melissa encouraged me to make an arrangement with another couple to pay them for meals on the days she was back on her undergraduate campus. At the seminary dormitory for married couples, we all shared a community kitchen. So my eating with another couple did not involve my having to invade their apartment, and it provided company for me during the periods when Melissa was not at home.

No couple lives happily without both a high level of interpersonal skills and a great deal of luck. The salient skills include coping, problem solving, and superior communication. Since both Melissa and I were trained as professional counselors (she in psychiatric nursing and I in counseling psychology), we had plenty of opportunity to learn communication skills.

We are also both rather good at problem solving, although our styles are different. I tend first to react to a conflict by seeing myself as the superior one, and (sometimes directly, often indirectly) implying that she is the one who needs to change. But after I've vented some anger, I frequently realize my own role in the conflict. Melissa tends to blame herself first, then gradually recognize that we both have a part in the conflict, which she then tries to resolve through her own problem-solving techniques. I need to deal with the emotional aspects before I can see the need for compromise or the possibility of a new approach.

In our early years together these differences sometimes resulted in a period of stalemate. I would often express my frustration in a way that implied she was to blame. Melissa would tend to lose hope in the communication. She would close the door to the bedroom of our two-room apartment, in order to take a break from our interaction. I would desperately try to continue to communicate, even if the process was going in circles. I had trouble letting go of an argument or conflict, and would hang on like a pit bull, while she needed space to settle down and think it through.

Several hours after one of these episodes, when we

had cooled down and felt sure our communication wouldn't escalate into another conflict, we agreed to sit down and try to understand each other's reactions. Melissa explained that in her parents' home, anger was displayed only in the most subtle ways. Now, living with me, when she saw me express anger more directly, it scared her. To feel safe and to cool down, she needed to stop the interaction and be alone. I explained that when she closed the door it felt to me like total rejection. I was not used to an interaction's being abruptly cut off with no resolution. Total silence, plus not even being able to see each other, felt to me like being abandoned.

Although I don't recall the exact sequence, I think we both genuinely tried to understand each other's behaviors and the emotions behind them. We weren't quite sure what we could do differently that would work for both of us, but we agreed to experiment. We promised that the next time we argued we would experiment with taking a break and then share what the experience was like for each of us. Like most attempts to change behavior in times of conflict, it did not go perfectly, but each of us was able to credit the other with trying to improve the process, and eventually we discovered ways to make facing our differences much more tolerable. Our different backgrounds and ways of reacting did not prevent us from continuing to live together. I realized that the rejection or isolation I felt was temporary and did not threaten the depth of our love for each other.

By spring of 1964 we were both excited about my finishing my seminary degree and Melissa's finishing her nursing work in Rochester and starting her master's degree in psychiatric nursing. I also wanted to go on for a doctoral degree, but we weren't sure if we could both be students again or whether it was my turn to work full time. Several metropolitan areas in the US had at least one or two universities that offered the degrees each of us wanted next. Fairly early in our application process, Melissa got word that she had been accepted in a new specialized nursing master's program at Boston University and would receive a grant that would pay all her expenses – tuition, room and board!

This was a wonderful offer, so she committed herself to that program. I had already applied to the doctoral program at Boston University; now I hedged my bets and applied to master's programs in pastoral counseling in the Boston area as well. Initially I received bad news: I was rejected for the doctoral program at B.U. This was a blow to my ego and to my assumption that I was academically superior to Melissa. The graduate pastoral counseling program at the nearby Andover-Newton seminary seemed like the best second choice for me, but on the day of my interviews I was so anxious about rejection that I was vomiting. Nonetheless, I made it through.

I was accepted into both master's programs: Boston University's and Andover Newton's. Soon I was offered a job teaching in the Human Relations department of Boston University's School of Business, so I committed to Boston University with the plan to reapply for the doctoral program after I had gotten to know some of the professors there. I deliberately registered for courses taught by professors who were involved in admission decisions in the doctoral program. I believed when these professors got to know me and my academic work, they'd recognize that I was doctoral material.

Late in the summer we made the move from the Middle Atlantic states where both of us had spent most of our lives to New England, where we found a garret apartment on the third floor of a beautiful old family home in a suburb of Boston.

CHAPTER 8
BISEXUALITY DAWNS

The classes I taught at Boston University were small enough for me to get to know each individual and to focus on the personal changes occurring in these students. It was the kind of teaching I cared about: integrating academic knowledge with personal development. I loved being a catalyst for others' growth.

The University was a Methodist institution, but the move to Boston turned out to be the end of my affiliation with Methodism. Melissa and I began to explore different churches in Boston's west suburbs. I was seriously interested in the United Church of Christ (UCC) as a denomination in which I might be ordained. We discovered Eliot Church in nearby Newton, only a few miles from our apartment. The building was a traditional New England church: red bricks, a Greek facade of white columns supporting a frieze, and a tall white steeple. The sanctuary walls were white, with stained wooden pews and plain glass windows letting in plenty of light. The Rev. Harold Fray was a stimulating speaker, a caring pastor, and a courageous and prophetic activist. The open-mindedness of the UCC and the social activism of the congregation fit well with the style of ministry I imagined myself doing. Unlike Methodism, UCC did not use creeds in worship, and its organizational structure required congregational representatives to deal face to face with the minister if there were criticisms or conflicts.

I contacted the area UCC board that screened candidates for ordination. When I met with them, I found them open to a wide range of theological orientations; they accepted my mixture of liberal theology and commitment

I Took Both Roads

to social justice. I had found a congregation and a denominational home that were a good fit for both my beliefs and my doubts. In August 1966 Melissa's parents, my own parents, and other friends and relatives came to Newton to celebrate my ordination in Eliot Church.

The solid sense of acceptance I felt from the church, the ordination council, and eventually from Boston University's pastoral counseling program laid the foundations for a different, more mature direction for my ministry: integrating teaching, counseling, and social action. I began to focus more on inclusiveness, in terms of theology and of minority groups. Later my understanding of inclusiveness broadened to include persons of all sexual orientations and all religions. 3

I occasionally attended the Arlington Street Unitarian Universalist (UU) church in Boston's historic old town. I was impressed with the ministry of the Rev. Jack Mendelsohn. The Rev. James Reeb had been associated with this church. He was murdered while involved in civil rights work in Selma, Alabama in March 1965, and I attended a memorial service in his honor at Arlington Church. Two of my seminary friends in Rochester had been Unitarian Universalists, and I shared their liberal theology and inclusive attitudes. These experiences, in seminary and in Boston, sowed the seeds for my later joining the Unitarian Universalist denomination.

~ ~ ~

In January of 1965, after one semester at Boston University, I was accepted into the doctoral program and a year and a half later became a pastoral counseling fellow. This group provided free psychotherapy to clients from the community. We met weekly in intensive individual and group supervision with two excellent mentors, Dr. Homer Jernigan and Dr. John Maes. All fourteen fellows were doctoral candidates chosen for our potential to become clinician scholars. My acceptance into this group both validated and challenged me: never before had I been in a group of men who seemed sure of themselves academically, personally, and physically.

Do any of these graduate students feel emotionally insecure about their ability to succeed? I wondered. *And do any of them feel insecure about their masculinity, the way I do? If they do, they sure don't show it!*

Fortunately, there were two aspects of being on the pastoral counseling service staff that reassured me. First, my supervisors were open about their own lives and were very accepting. They not only expected self-disclosure and personal growth from us, but they modeled it as well.

Second, there was a high level of humor and camaraderie among both the students and professors in the group. Thanks to my father, I have always had a sense of humor, but what was new to me and felt so good was laughing *with* the group, not feeling outside it.

Still, I felt anxious during the group meetings. My supervisor Dr. Jernigan encouraged me to start therapy, pointing out that many counselors found it useful to go through the process themselves. He connected me with Dr. Gordon. Not long afterwards, I dreamt about my new therapist – the dream that brought my first awareness that I was sexually attracted to men.

As I tried to face my newfound sexual interests, I was convinced that this would not mean the end of my sexual and loving attraction to Melissa. Looking back on my life, it's clear that sexuality was not the only area in which I have chosen to take both paths. Many times, instead of deciding between two contrasting elements, I have enjoyed exploring both paths and affirming both. Perhaps it's a central theme in my identity, although I didn't know it at that time.

I hate choices that imply exclusivity. Much of life is

NOT a zero-sum game. When you win on one side, you do not necessarily lose on the other. When you affirm your need to be alone at times (introversion), that may actually increase your ability to be genuinely present with other people, to be extraverted, at other times. When you love men, it doesn't necessarily mean you don't love women.

~ ~ ~

Sitting at the table in our tiny kitchen, Melissa and I shared fantasies for our future and planned our next moves. Soon she would graduate from her master's program, ready to begin her new profession as a mental health nurse. The timing was good. The nation's first comprehensive mental health center was to be built in Lowell, Massachusetts, about an hour's drive from Boston University. Beginning in the fall of 1966, Melissa became the Supervisor of Nursing for inpatient psychiatric care, working part-time in the primarily outpatient clinic as well. It was a big step up.

By that fall I had completed most of my class work and needed to be on the Boston U. campus only a couple of days a week. We moved to Lowell, and I secured a part-time faculty position in the Psychology Department at Fitchburg State College. We couldn't afford two cars, so we rented an apartment on Malden Avenue within walking or biking distance from the Lowell Mental Health Center. Melissa could get to work even if I was commuting by car to Fitchburg State or to Boston U.

We moved into the first floor apartment of the small two-flat house. A newly married couple, Dave and Olga Firth, lived above us. They were from working-class backgrounds, with no college experience.

We first had a chance to socialize on the Fourth of July when the four of us went together to a nearby carnival. Melissa and Olga sat on a bench talking, while Dave and I rode the Ferris wheel together. But before we had finished the ride, Dave developed a splitting headache – so severe that we all returned to the house early.

Dave soon became so sick he couldn't work. Tests showed that he had a tumor in his brain. Olga had to go to work full time in order to support them and maintain their health insurance coverage; there was no way they could afford home nursing care.

By then I had collected most of the data for my doctoral dissertation. I was focused on writing up my thesis, but I could do that from our home. So I offered to stay with Dave during the hours Olga was at work. I would sit on Dave and Olga's sun porch in the apartment above our own, working on my writing.

After several operations, Dave realized that his brain cancer had become incurable. His crew cut did not hide the scars from his previous brain surgery, two curving lines on the left side of his skull. Most of our conversations were not about his health, but about Melissa's new job, or what I was writing in my thesis, or our cars, or other practical things. On one level we had little in common, but we found it comfortable to chat and be together.

Why does God allow a young man like Dave to die? I wondered. *Why will He soon force Olga to live as a widow, without the man she loves dearly?* But Dave was a simple workingman and did not seem to question things or argue with God or with the facts of his life. He was in and out of the hospital several times. He became increasingly disabled by the tumor, which began to affect his ability to stand up or walk and often caused serious headaches.

Gradually, I became more of a nurse's aide rather than just someone to keep him company. We knew, after several operations and hospitalizations, that the cancer was continuing to grow, producing pressure in Dave's skull. Nothing more could be done, and there was no reason for him not to live out his remaining days at home.

He slept more and more. Often I sat on their porch, listening to be sure Dave was OK in the nearby bedroom. When he was awake he would call out to me if he wanted anything, sometimes a drink of water or just wanting to talk. Most of the time he was relaxed. But occasionally he would wake up startled, suddenly afraid to be alone. I was thankful that I had outgrown my earlier difficulties in relating to those less educated than I. I was glad I could be company for Dave, and that I could assist him physically when he needed help getting to the toilet or dressing. I knew that touch between men can be can be caring and comforting without being sexual.

One sunny day, I heard Dave call out to me. There was an urgency in his voice. I rushed into the room and sat beside him on the bed.

Dave sat upright, startled – his headache so painful that tears welled up in his eyes. He seemed unable to speak. He turned to me and reached out with both arms, and we embraced. It struck me: *He knows he's about to die.* I felt a deep warmth and compassion for him. He struggled to say something. All I could catch was the word "Olga," his wife's name. I wondered if he was confused and thought he was hugging his wife. *It doesn't matter*, I said to myself. His hug was desperate, hanging on to life, not wanting to be alone.

Then gradually his muscles relaxed. I continued to hug him as he grew weaker, his breathing gradually growing gentler and gentler until it stopped. I held him tenderly until all life drained out of his body, he became limp, and his eyes closed. I laid him back down, knowing he was dead, but feeling close to him and calm.

There was nothing violent about Dave's death. It was so peaceful and the contact so real that I was grateful that we had been together. It took a while to realize that he was gone and to feel a gentle sadness about it. This was a holy event.

~ ~ ~

I stood in Boston University's open plaza on Commonwealth Avenue, immediately in front of Marsh Chapel. Students were arriving from all directions, most of them with suitcases, duffle bags, and other luggage. We were waiting for the chartered buses which would carry us all the way to Raleigh, North Carolina.

For over a decade, since my senior year in high school, the race problem had been tugging on my conscience. It seemed so clear, a black and white issue of equality and justice. It was years later that I recognized that I had a personal stake in this issue of equality, that I was also a member of a minority group. The obvious connection between these two struggles for civil rights – rights for Blacks and rights for Gays – was not acknowledged by either major political party until forty years later, in Barak Obama's stirring speech at the Democratic Convention of 2008.

Liberation had come to be the central theme in my ministry, both personal liberation – freeing the self from illusions and enhancing self-knowledge – and social liberation of minority groups, leading from oppression to freedom and justice. Action, not belief, was my creed.

It is easy to misperceive the nature of work for social justice. The drama that makes the TV news belies the fact that much of social activism consists of pure grunt work. It is as repetitious and low key as most factory jobs.

But there are also occasions of breakthrough, occasions when the barriers between groups of people break down and humanity is recognized as one. Those are the occasions we remember all of our lives. It is in those events that social activism becomes a gateway to the sacred. Our work in Raleigh was one of those occasions.

We worked in the black ghettos in pairs consisting of a black college student, usually from Raleigh or nearby, and a white college student, sometimes from far away. Although I worked with different teammates each day, in each case I felt a new sense of how urgent getting out the Negro vote was to those students. I also felt their appreciation for the white students' involvement as comrades in the fight. After days of working together, the students bonded. Just before those of us from Boston got on the bus to go home, the whole group formed a circle. Black and white together, arms over each other's shoulders, we sang "We Shall Overcome" with a passion I'd never before experienced. We were all in tears, partly because we northerners hated to leave, and partly because we all knew the danger to which the North Carolina youth would continue to be exposed. But most of all, we felt united in the cause of justice, as brothers and sisters, fully believing that where one person is denied justice we all suffer.

For me, this experience of integrating my theological and pastoral training with social action was a more important culminating event than the graduation ceremony in which I received my PhD. My values of inclusion and liberation were incarnated in action.

CHAPTER 9
THE RURAL MIDWEST

After I had completed my doctorate, Melissa and I had two criteria for choosing our next place to live. I searched for a college that encouraged innovative teaching, a place where I could connect with students at both academic and personal levels. It had to be in a community where Melissa could practice mental health or pediatric nursing. I learned that a small liberal arts college, Marietta College in southeastern Ohio, was developing a new psychology department. Dr. Al Prince, a strict behaviorist, had been hired to as chair. He was seeking a humanistic psychologist to teach the "soft" courses, which he did not consider scientific. I liked the idea of helping to build a new academic department. But I also wanted to make use of my counseling skills, so I set up a meeting with the head of the student counseling service, Dr. Margaret Ross. A pleasant and creative woman, she was delighted by the possibility of having a male counselor to complement her work. (Many students are more comfortable seeing a counselor of their own sex.) Margaret successfully lobbied the Dean to hire me half time in counseling, half in psychology.

Some weeks later Melissa and I traveled to Marietta to look for housing. We had dreaded leaving New England's rocky coast and beautiful mountains. But to our delight, a few miles out of the college town we discovered a house situated on a small hill with a panoramic view of the surrounding hills and valleys, foothills to the Appalachian Mountains. In midsummer we loaded our three rooms of furniture into a trailer and headed to our new home.

It took us a couple of days to unpack. When that was

finished, about dusk the third day, I walked across the road to introduce myself to our nearest neighbor. As I approached his house, a gruff man's voice shouted out, "I've got you covered!"

"I'm just your new neighbor," I shouted back, as calmly as I could. When I got closer I stretched out both arms in his direction, showing that I was not armed, and reached out my right hand to shake his. He shifted his gun to his left hand, shook my hand, and said, "A stranger shouldn't approach a house at night."

I knew that farmers owned guns for hunting, and I had shot woodchucks on my grandpa's farm and watched my uncle use a gun to kill a pig for slaughter. But I'd never thought of farmers' guns as weapons to kill humans. And I'd never thought of myself as an aggressor. So it was a shock to be viewed as a threat to a neighbor. But to Mr. Phillips, I wasn't yet a neighbor; I was a stranger.

He was friendly enough after he got to know us. When he retired from farming, he invited me over to his house to show me to the cozy extra room he'd just had built. His best view, like ours, was to the northwest – but he had the new window installed facing southwest, where graded land rose upwards and blocked the scenic view. He had spent his life subduing nature to feed his livestock and his family. From his perspective, nature was something to struggle against, not beautiful scenery to enjoy.

These were just the first of the many cultural differences we would encounter as we transitioned from a large university city to a small college town. My experiences in my grandparents' farm community helped me relate to our neighbors and some of my colleagues. And I remembered the genuine caring of many adults I'd experienced in the small community in which I had grown up. Nevertheless, I was conscious of how different my view of the world had become during my twelve years of interacting with people from various ethnic groups, nations, and races. I also realized how hard it was for me to keep an open mind when confronted with adults who assumed that their way was the only right way.

~ ~ ~

I believe in teaching experientially. But most students who enrolled in my classes expected the classroom experience to be cognitive; they did not anticipate that it would challenge them emotionally. My course in Adolescent Psychology offered students opportunities to deal with their own identity formation by voluntarily joining a small sharing group. Nothing that happened in this group would affect their grade in the course.

My work in the college counseling service also included experiential learning, co-facilitating a structured freshmen orientation process that Dr. Ross had implemented a year before my arrival. During orientation week, each incoming freshman student was assigned to a discussion group of six to eight students led by a trained upper-class student supervised by either Margaret or myself. The structured groups discussed a different topic each week. Margaret recognized that freshmen students on residential campuses undergo a life-changing experience, moving away from their families and former friends into a new environment. [4] They need to build a new network of friends. She had designed the discussion groups to help new students develop deeper relationships with their classmates.

In the supervision meetings, we encouraged the group leaders to share not only what was happening in their group but also what they were experiencing emotionally. As they sought to help the freshmen, they frequently found some of their own issues emerging. The meetings fostered the personal growth of the student leaders, just as these leaders were fostering growth in the freshman.

I found that my dual roles of counselor and a professor in this secular college fulfilled my desire to minister to students personally and experientially, not just cognitively.

My interactions with these student leaders were personal and often developed into mentorships, and sometimes into friendships. I particularly remember a somewhat hippie-ish young man named Ron Reese who brought out the playful child in me. It was clear we both enjoyed each other. One bright spring day I spotted Ron across the quad, and started skipping my way toward him. (It's not particularly common to see professors skipping on campus). He responded gleefully, and ran up and hugged me. It was a joy to be interacting in playful ways, rather than predictable roles. The hippie movement and student activism were having a positive influence even on this rural Midwest campus.

~ ~ ~

When Melissa and I had begun to settle into our Marietta home, we sought out a new spiritual community. But the United Church of Christ nearby did not seem to have either inclusive theology or social action. We had to look beyond the denomination in which I had been ordained.

Sunday after Sunday we visited new churches, attending both the worship service and the adult religious education class. We asked people who greeted us, "Are any of you in a group that supports your own spiritual and personal development?" No such groups seemed to exist in this area. Often someone we met would request, "If you find such a group, be sure to call me. I'd like to be in one too." We decided to found one ourselves. We collected names of those who were interested and invited them to attend the first meeting of a spiritual support group to be held in our home. Over twenty people arrived! They included three former nuns, a Catholic priest, several ministers, counselors and social workers, college faculty, and others. The group met for well over a year. It became a powerful support and a major force in our own spiritual growth. It was a lesson for us both: if you can't find what you need, initiate it.

~ ~ ~

With both of us now settled in our careers and in our college town, my longing to raise children re-emerged. Melissa agreed to try. We stopped using birth control, but almost a year went by with no pregnancy.

We had settled on a back-up plan: to adopt children, most likely children of color. We applied to an agency in Athens, Ohio, a university town about an hour from Marietta, and stipulated that since we expected to spend most of our lives in academic settings, we wanted a child who was likely to become "college material" (as much as that could be predicted). We were open to a child of any race and gender. We knew that biracial children were hard to place. In 1970 most black parents who were applying to adopt only wanted black children – and most white parents wanted white children.

So it was no surprise to us that, soon after we were approved as potential parents, we were notified that a biracial baby boy was available. Both of his parents were college students, and both were musical; they played in a jazz band together. His birth mother was white; his birth father was black. We took this baby boy into our home when he was only six weeks old. Our new son, whom we named Nathan, was a strong and active infant but seemed to have every allergy in the books. It was a good thing that Melissa was a nurse!

My mother and father had already had four grandchildren when Lucille and her husband Bob had adopted a son who was black, so the issue of interracial adoption was not new to my parents. They seemed to accept and respond to our adopted biracial kids with the same outgoing affection that they showed toward their other grandchildren.

It was harder for Melissa's folks to deal with the fact that Nathan was biracial. A year before we brought Nathan home, Mom Sundberg learned of my sister Lucille's adopted black son, and asked us, "You two wouldn't do something like that, would you?"

Melissa guessed that one issue for her parents was "What will the neighbors think?" So before we brought Nathan to their home, Melissa asked her parents if they would be more comfortable coming to our home to see their grandson. But instead, they chose to have us come to them. Nathan was extremely hyperactive while we were there. We had to build a fence around the Christmas tree to preserve it. But Melissa's parents did their best to be supportive.

Less than a year later we got an unexpected phone call from the adoption agency. "We know you were planning to wait a couple of years and then adopt a baby girl. But we have an eleven-month-old biracial girl right now. We do NOT want to place her in a third foster home."

When we met Michelle, she already knew her name, so we did not change it. She was petite, cute, and already walking. She was several shades darker than Nathan, but, like him, she was the child of two college students, a black father and a white mother.

Having two children only three months apart in age was much like raising twins. But their personalities were very different. Nathan needed constant stimulation, and Michelle was outgoing and sociable, so having Michelle around actually seemed to make Nathan happier.

Whatever reservations Mom and Dad Sundberg had about our adopted biracial children, they did their best to be good grandparents.

David R. Matteson

One of my favorite memories of raising biracial children occurred around the dining room table when the kids were about five. It was late summer, and Nathan was commenting on how we each looked different.

"In the winter, I'm tan, Michelle is brown, Mommy is white, and Daddy is white. In the summer, both Michelle and I are brown, Mommy is tan, and Daddy is pink.

"Now I have a flat nose and Michelle has a flat nose. Daddy has a pointy nose and Mommy has a pointy nose. But when we grow up I will have a pointy nose, and Michelle will have a pointy nose. We all will have pointy noses!"

Since Michelle's complexion is considerably darker than Nathan's, it is much more obvious that she has African-American lineage. I took her with me to visit my Dad's only sibling, my Aunt Lu, a single woman in her early 60's at the time. Aunt Lu was still living in Pennsylvania near the farm on which she and my dad had grown up. Everyone within many miles of that village was Caucasian, so if Aunt Lu had ever seen a black person it was only on TV, and probably was Sammy Davis Jr.

Michelle was quite a sociable toddler, and after Aunt Lu had offered her some cookies, Michelle walked over to where Aunt Lu was seated and reached up her arms asking to be lifted onto her lap. Michelle was too charming to resist, and after an hour or less, Aunt Lu and Michelle had become friends.

When we were ready to leave, Aunt Lu stood by my car window and thanked me for coming.

"And thanks for bringing Michelle to see me. She is such a sweet little girl," she said. "And she can't help it that she's black."

Each of us overcomes our prejudices in little steps, one at a time. This applies to prejudice against homosexuality as well as race, and is one of the reasons I believe it is important for me – and those of other "invisible" minorities – to come out to people who already have some sense of me as a person but don't realize that I happen to be bisexual.

~ ~ ~

After teaching for five years at Marietta College, I had applied for and been granted a year's sabbatical. Melissa and I decided to spend the academic year 1973-74 in Denmark.

Only weeks before leaving for Europe, I attended a conference in Cleveland and, after the day's meetings and dinner, I decided to look for a gay bar. Was it synchronicity that the person I sat next to at the bar happened to be European?

Franz, on the bar stool to my left, waited till I ordered a glass of wine. Then he turned to me and introduced himself. I knew his accent was European, although I couldn't identify what country he was from. I mentioned that, in a few weeks, I would be leaving for my first trip to Europe and would be living there for fourteen months. Franz told me that he had grown up in Austria. I admitted that I knew relatively little about this area. Realizing I was genuinely interested in learning about other cultures, Franz talked about Austria and its contribution to classical music: the waltzes of Strauss and the symphonies of Mozart, Haydn, and Mahler. After some small talk about museums and famous works of art, ever so gracefully Franz shifted the conversation to something more immediate.

"You know, sitting at this gay bar here in America is very different from sitting at a gay bar in Austria. If we were in Vienna, here on the bar in front of each of us would be a candle – unlit, but waiting for one of us to light it. And, let's say I was attracted to you, and I wanted you to know it but I didn't want to be offensive or too assertive. I would take my cigarette lighter and light your candle. And if you were Austrian, you'd know that what I meant by that was that I was interested in you. Now, if you were tired and did not want anything more, you would politely continue the conversation, but as you were doing so, you would quietly snuff out the candle, indicating you weren't interested." He paused.

I said, "So I would realize that your lighting the candle was a pleasant invitation; that you were willing to take the initiative, perhaps sensing that I'm new at this. I would have no inclination to snuff out the candle."

He smiled. "I don't live far from here. You have a car?"

I nodded.

"You could follow me home. There will be nothing assumed other than that we might have another drink of wine if you like, and we could sleep in my double bed, and absolutely nothing more would happen unless you were comfortable with it."

Franz's subtlety and gentleness, and his cultured yet unimposing manner, made me feel comfortable. It seemed so exciting and generous.

I accepted his offer, and we enjoyed a single glass of wine together at his home. Then we snuggled in bed together, which led to enjoying beautiful but non-penetrating sex together. It was very exciting, and yet wonderfully relaxed. I could hardly believe I felt so comfortable with him, so at home doing what was very new to me.

When I woke up in the morning he had already headed off to work, as he had forewarned me. He had left the makings of breakfast for me. After showering and eating, I headed back to the conference center for the next day of professional meetings.

But by the time I arrived, I was feeling split. The gay experience felt like coming home – and yet, being with

Melissa also felt like home. In fact, it WAS home. How could both be home?

I decide to call Melissa to be honest with her about this momentous event in my life. When she answered, I blurted out the outline of the night's events, excited and happy, and wanting her to share in it. But Melissa began to cry.

"I know you're being honest, and I thank you for that," she said sadly. "But I can't handle this over the phone. I wish you'd just waited till you got home to tell me."

As I hung up, I felt bad that, in my rush to tell her, I had been insensitive. At the same time, I was relieved that she was not feeling judgmental. I felt sure that we could work this out. Somehow I was confident that my emerging queerness, although it seemed like a revolutionary change in who I was, could not destroy our marriage. I knew that our love was real. It couldn't suddenly end, just because a new part of me suddenly had begun.

Although Melissa, in the ensuing years, regularly worried that I might leave her to live with a man, my worry was the reverse – that she might find that her love for me was more painful than it was worth, that she might leave me to live on her own or with a man who was straight and could live with her as his only sexual partner.

~ ~ ~

We needed time and trusted friends to sort out the implications of my newly discovered bisexuality. Melissa and I decided to make a trip to the Toronto area where close friends from our Boston University days, Garth and Dorothy Mundle, were living. Melissa deeply trusted Garth, and I sensed that Garth was comfortable with the gay issue. I was sure that Dorothy would be concerned but not judgmental.

And my expectations were correct. Garth and Dorothy were both trained in Christian ministries in the United

David R. Matteson

Church of Canada, Garth as an ordained pastor and Dorothy as a diaconal minister (pastoral care and education). They were both empathetic toward Melissa and the fears my newfound bisexuality evoked in her. But they also were comfortable with my new understanding of my own sexual orientation and welcomed discussing it.

The UC of Canada supported the inclusion of les-bi-gays within the Christian church. For most UC Canada ministers, the central message of Christianity was the overarching, unmerited love of God, and the words of scripture were seen in historic context rather than as inerrant. So the homophobia associated with some parts of Christianity was not an issue with these friends.

I was interested in Toronto for another reason. For some time I had subscribed to Toronto's *Body Politic*, one of the best gay newspapers of that period. I wanted to meet some of the columnists whose writing showed that they were comfortable being "out" at this early stage of North America's gay rights movement. Meeting them in 1973 was extremely helpful for me. It was only four years after the les-bi-gay-trans rebellion at the Stonewall bar in Greenwich Village, New York City, yet these journalists were already very comfortable being openly gay. They were real-life examples that being gay is not something pathological and that affirming it can lead to a healthy identity.

It's a risky business to be open about one's queerness – not to mention being open about one's extramarital involvements. We did not share it with anyone where we lived then. Washington County, Ohio had supported Barry Goldwater for President. Except for some belonging to the University and members of the Unitarian Universalist Church, most of the community was politically and religiously conservative. We suspected they were also socially conservative.

I Took Both Roads

Perhaps I felt a bit freer while teaching far from home during the five summers we spent in Bemidji, Minnesota. Although I did not directly come out about being bisexual myself, in the ethics portion of the section of Introduction to Psychology that I taught to nurses I included material on their professional duty to provide equal care to gays and lesbians and their visiting partners or lovers.

CHAPTER 10
SCANDINAVIA

For my sabbatical year in Copenhagen, a local professor of psychology hired me to conduct his lectures at a teachers' college while he was away at speaking engagements in continental Europe. Besides allowing me to experience work life in Danish culture, this meant that we would be able to live there without having to go in debt. But there were other issues.

"You will be working regularly at the teachers' college," Melissa pointed out, "so you'll have a chance to get to know other professors and develop your own social life. But at least until I get the kids settled into some kind of pre-school, I won't have any adult social support but you."

Melissa knew that one reason I was so excited about living in Denmark was because it is the only country in the Western world that was not influenced by Puritanism. In the mid-1970s, gay liberation was much further along in Scandinavia and the Netherlands than in North America.

"I'm comfortable with you meeting and getting to know gay men living in Denmark – but remember, I won't have those same chances, at least at first. You can develop friendships with some of these men if you want to. But please promise me you won't get sexually involved with them."

As usual, Melissa stated her needs without any condemnation of my own wishes and longings. I committed to limiting my friendships to platonic ones.

During my undergraduate years, one of my closest college friends had been an Icelandic student, Oli Hoskuldsson. Melissa and I decided that, on our way to continental Europe, we should spend a few days visiting Oli and his family in Iceland.

At that time, Oli and his wife had two sons who were preschoolers, like our own two children. Besides enjoying this wonderful country and Oli's delightful family, staying in their home provided a chance for our children to experience being with children who did not speak English. For young children, language is of secondary importance; they played together beautifully. Meanwhile Oli and I caught up, and both Melissa and I enjoyed getting to know his wife Bylgja. Our whole family was fascinated by the abundant geothermal heat and the joys of hot springs in the midst of the winter-like climate.

Oli's brother was the warden of Iceland's major prison, so he showed me around. One of the most interesting aspects of the tour was a conversation with one of the top staff. As I was being introduced to the facility, I asked a staff member if conjugal visitation was allowed.

I had read that many Scandinavian prisons not only allowed the prisoner's wife or primary partner to visit, but set up the visits in a private room with a double bed, so that the couple were free to have sex. Oli translated my question into Icelandic. The response was, "Of course we wouldn't deny a prisoner the right to have sex with his partner; that would be inhumane!"

"Of course," indeed! This was a wonderful introduction to the humanitarian Scandinavian attitudes toward sexuality, rooted in a belief in human redemption, rather than punishment.

I was on target in choosing Scandinavia as the place to test my ideas, not just on gender roles, but on sexuality, I thought to myself.

When we arrived in Denmark, we stayed briefly in several of the beautiful old farmhouses that had been converted into "holiday farms," homes where a guest family can spend a week or more in the country. Usually the upper story of the farmhouse had been transformed into an apartment where the visitors could sleep and have time alone; the farm family provided the meals. In our case, we had chosen families who had children about the same age as Nathan and Michelle.

One warm summer day, the farm children got out a garden hose and turned on a sprayer. Soon all four kids were running through the spray of cooling water, giggling. The Danish children chattered in Danish, and Michelle and Nathan chattered back in English. Although they didn't understand each other's words, there was no barrier to their acceptance and joy. Is this what Jesus meant about becoming like children? Would that gays and straights could do the same!

Our second holiday farm was near the beach. Most of the Danish families enjoyed swimming in the nude. It was simply a way to enjoy the ocean. Men and women of all body types seemed comfortable being in the nude. I particularly remember Michelle, with her dark complexion and frizzy black hair, parading around in the nude. She was a stark visual contrast to the blonde, light-skinned Danes. More than once, our charming three-year-old daughter would entrance some tall blonde Danish man. The Danes tend to be more extraverted and expressive than Swedes or Norwegians. One man reached down and spontaneously picked Michelle up and held her in his arms seven feet or more above the ground, telling her, in Danish, what a cute, unique little brown girl she was! It's astonishing how accurately children are able to read body-language; despite Michelle's early fear of men, she did not seem to be frightened by this tall but warm-hearted Dane.

On the beach, we became comfortable seeing women's exposed breasts, so it was less of a surprise when we eventually arrived in Copenhagen to see women topless, sunning in their yards. Mothers on buses and trains openly nursed their babies – something perfectly natural but almost unknown in US at that time. *Are we back in the Garden of Eden*, I thought, *where we are not ashamed of our bodies, and know them to be God's creation?*

In Copenhagen, I began to explore the gay culture. My commitment not to have gay sexual involvements was not difficult; in fact, it fit my style at that stage of my life. There was so much to learn, and I found it fascinating listening to the stories of men who had gone through their own coming out and dealt with their parents and siblings. I immersed myself in one of my favorite endeavors, the process of understanding another culture. I didn't need the added stimulation of sexual involvements.

While in Denmark I began writing the first book in adolescent psychology to clarify the differences between male and female identity development (Matteson, 1975). Since many women professors were frustrated by typical textbooks that generalized from studies based solely on male samples, they adopted my book as a supplementary text.

In addition to my formal research, Melissa and I enjoyed discussing with Danish couples their methods of raising children. Nathan and Michelle's presence made it easy for us to socialize with Scandinavian couples with young children. We were fascinated by the low aggression and more mature behavior of Danish children compared to American kids, so we continually asked questions.

The year flew by with no threats to our marriage, despite the fact that Scandinavia was much more sexually liberated than our own culture. I was impressed that Denmark was every bit as democratic as the United States and far more humane and tolerant. The experience of living there helped me see American culture more clearly.

As my sabbatical year neared its end, we made a

David R. Matteson

wonderful tour through Europe. We loaded our bright red English station wagon onto a ferry to East Germany and then drove through what was then rural Czechoslovakia, under Soviet rule. With our "colored" kids and our colorful car, we were the center of attention in an area where kids were pure white and cars were black, grey or navy blue.

One evening, after a meal in a small town restaurant, our waiter came running out after us. *We must have left one of the kids' toys on the table*, I thought. But instead the waiter handed me a shot glass, crystal with a gold rim, as a spontaneous gift. Passionately, with tears in his eyes, he declared in broken English, "We love you Americans." As much as I admired Scandinavian culture, I suddenly felt proud of how the USA was seen as the exemplar of freedom.

Not all Europeans saw us so positively. In Switzerland, after a long car ride, Nathan began to run around playfully in a meadow. Suddenly a man screamed from a house on an adjoining property "Are you Americans?"

A little surprised by his this question, I answered, "Yes, we are."

To which he screamed louder, "Tell that boy meadows are to look at, not to play in."

It was a rude transition from the fun-loving, child-affirming Danish attitudes to the regimented and ordered values of the Swiss. But I was grateful he had yelled at me, as the parent, rather than scolding my son.

How do we best deal with cultures whose values are at odds with our own? If we value freedom for all, but another culture views homosexuality as a sin, does it have the right to impose restrictions on gay sex? If Swiss culture sees discipline as a higher goal than emotional expression and spontaneity, is screaming at a child a form of child abuse, or a form of education?

I had been prepared for the culture shock of going

overseas. But the difficulty of re-entry into American culture was a surprise! Perhaps it was because so many of my values were more aligned with those of Scandinavian culture. Maybe the shock waves on returning were reverberations from the shattering of a myth: the belief that United States is the most democratic of nations. I agreed whole-heartedly with a statement attributed to St. Augustine: "The world is a book, and those who do not travel read only one page."

I had learned a lot in Scandinavia. I was about to learn even more.

CHAPTER 11
BEING THE BOSS

I had a new job as the director of the Community Mental Health Center of Washington County. It was my first experience as an administrator and the center's first experience with a full-time director.

I was counseling and supervising other counselors, both of which I'd done in previous jobs. But in addition, I was now spending hour after hour signing papers and filling out forms. I had to learn about new state regulations, rules from the agency board, and different rules from the country mental health board – both of which had power over the Mental Health Center. The two boards were frequently in conflict with each other, and I was in the middle.

I had never had power over others at work before, except in minor ways as a dormitory counselor and as a professor. I now had the responsibility of evaluating staff and of hiring and firing.

My inexperience and the pressures of the job led to a serious error in judgment. Greta, who had served as acting director during our year abroad, had alienated most of the clinical staff. I observed her interactions with them for a month or so, and without consulting the two boards, I fired her. Members of both boards were shocked and angry.

Fortunately, Dr. Eleonore Krebs, a sensitive and creative school psychologist serving on the county board, calmly showed me how I had failed to respect Greta's good intentions and dedicated service. My intervening without consulting the boards, although legal, had been a mistake in strategy. With Eleonore's help, I was able to acknowledge my blunder and work out a plan: I would apologize to Greta for wronging her and offer to reinstate her. This would validate the service she had given and at least allow her to save face.. If she agreed to return to her job, she would likely tone down any interactions she had with the clinical staff. I knew that admitting my error and following this school psychologist's suggestions was my best hope for limiting the damage.

Although I was relieved that Greta decided not to return, I was genuinely sorry I had hurt her and had so misjudged her contribution. My use of power closed off any chance of reconciliation.

But the most damaging aspect of my too precipitous rise to power was within our family. Nathan and Michelle were used to my being home when they returned from school. Now, working as an executive all day, I didn't arrive home until late evening. By then I was exhausted and longing for relaxation, while the kids needed my undivided attention. Especially with Nathan, I had become a study in the traditional male role. During this period, I was too preoccupied with supervision and administration to really understand Nathan's needs. In retrospect, I was expecting him to meet my demands, but I was not in tune with his.

Nathan was only four, and he was borderline ADD (attention deficit disorder). So he put his feelings into a striking physical demonstration. One morning when I was about to head off to the Mental Health Center, I saw Nathan run in front of the car, push against the hood, and try to stop my leaving.

Shaken, I got out of the driver's seat, picked him up, and hugged him tightly. I carried him to Melissa and then drove slowly out and headed to work. I couldn't quit the job that very moment, but part of me wanted to. Nathan's message was clear: Dad, if you come home and act like a tyrant, you will kill your relationship with me!

Although Melissa was good at helping me unwind when I returned home from the Mental Health Center, by that time she had been with the kids for several hours and wanted relief for herself. After a month or two of this pattern, Melissa once again told me that we needed to set aside some time for a serious talk. Melissa is extremely good at laying out a problem without blaming or criticizing, but this confrontation was hard for me. Despite all my investment in the Mental Health Center, I was not the traditional man getting all my ego satisfaction from my work. I had wanted children; I still wanted the children; and I still wanted to think of myself as a caring and nurturing father. But Melissa described how I repeatedly came home to a peaceful threesome (Melissa, Nathan and Michelle) and in a matter of minutes upset the kids just when they needed to settle down for bed.

After Melissa's description of my interactions with the children had begun to seep into my head and guts, she suggested a remedy: that I get out of the children's lives on weekday evenings! Of course she didn't state it that way; but that's the way it hit me.

"I want you to stay at the Center to continue your paperwork or to prepare for your teaching. When the kids are in bed and asleep, I will phone you to tell you it's OK to come home."

If I could take my ego out of the picture, this was a perfectly rational solution.

I can't say that I succeeded in placing my ego aside, but I really had no choice but to give the plan a try. When I got home later than usual that Monday evening, Melissa told me how much she appreciated it and that she was glad I was home. Gradually I realized that this pattern also helped me relax and unwind. I missed the kids, but I'm sure they didn't miss the upsetting evenings.

Thanks to Melissa's wisdom and her ability to share her perspective in non-judgmental ways, my experience of becoming a traditional male may have taught me as much about gender roles as did a year's observation of Danish culture, or several years of conducting and writing psychological research on masculinity.

After a while, I began to realize what I had been sacrificing for the sake of this administrative job. Although the feedback from the clinical staff was positive and the two boards wanted me to continue as Director, I knew there had to be some changes. Eventually I convinced the board to hire an assistant director to take over some of my duties. We were fortunate in finding a competent person, Mike Naylor, who worked well with me. But even with Mike's help, I gradually realized I was just not happy being an administrator. Probably no year of my adult life had been this difficult, yet taught me so much.

A few months later I started looking for job opportunities that would get me back into academia full time. The contrast between conservative Ohio and progressive Denmark made me long for a more liberal community. Race was an issue: our biracial children had had almost no chance to get to know other African-American or biracial children or adults. Racial and ethnic diversity became an important factor in looking for new jobs.

I was with Melissa and the kids on a much needed vacation on a lake when I got a phone call asking me to interview for a job at a new, innovative university south of Chicago.

When I arrived for the interview, the chair of the search committee, Dr. Bill Rogge, invited me to visit his class in human sexuality. He interviewed me for the academic job during the class. Students routinely were part of the decision process in hiring new professors here;

this was a unique University! But Bill was also a unique person, and to my surprise, in front of the class, he began to ask me personal questions about my sex life.

"Do you ever masturbate?" he asked.

"Of course," I answered.

At least he didn't ask me about homosexuality, I thought.

Later he asked me to do something odd or silly. I walked to the front of the class and stood on my head.

It's not surprising that many people in the area were skeptical about this new, unconventional university. It was one of the first to hold most classes in the late afternoon or evening and to teach classes in three-hour blocks so working students could make only one trip a week for a class. The neighborhood was an extension of one of the first totally planned suburbs, Park Forest. Sidewalks led through tunnels so children could skate or bike and never cross a heavily-trafficked road. Most important, the area had fought the phenomenon of "white flight" and matured into a community of stable racial integration. I found it a creative and exciting place.

I had once summarized my philosophy of education this way:

"My hope is that education will make the person's life a more fully human one, open to new possibilities of thinking and behavior, and thus more able to be wholly himself. Full humanness comes only with involvement in the real and personal world; education with this goal leads to involvement in society." (1968)

Now, at Governors State University, I would have an opportunity to live this philosophy.

Once again I was able to bargain for a double appointment: I joined both the counseling and the psychology departments. Melissa felt that living in the suburbs of a large metropolis would fit well with her own professional plans.

As it's turned out, Melissa and I have lived out the rest of our careers in this area. Thirteen years after moving to Chicago's south suburbs, our biracial children moved from our home to their respective undergrad colleges. Both of them thanked us for raising them in an integrated community, which had showed them that persons of different races can live together in safety and trust. My passion for teaching in ways that tapped the students' personal experience, and for living in a way that encouraged deep communication and development of friendships across racial and ethnic barriers, became a part of our day-to-day lives.

Of course, there were major adjustments to make. We had been living in areas where rolling hills and sailing lakes were nearby; the prairie landscape at first seemed flat and boring. Both Melissa's parents and mine had spent their whole lives in eastern states; now we were leaving them and our siblings to move hundreds of miles west. But we were sure it was the best move for the children and for me. It also turned out to be the beginning of Melissa's finding her own professional niche. In time, the move opened the way for Melissa to become a highly skilled nursing administrator.

CHAPTER 12
CHICAGO

It was wonderful to return to teaching and counseling, the work I loved. Governors State's focus on experiential learning excited me, and in my first year I learned much from Dr. Bill Rogge, now head of my department.

This was my first tenure track job in the counselor education field. My first book, *Adolescents Today: Sex Roles and the Search for Identity* (1975) had now been published, and the University bookstore sponsored a book signing, which added to my feeling of being welcomed to this new campus.

In that first year, two men on the faculty became important friends and role models. One was an attractive, sensuous, straight man named Rick Horowitz. I loved his wonderful sense of humor and spontaneous style. Although he was about twenty years younger and far more athletic than I, he invited me to run with him weekly. He was an excellent personal trainer as well as a fine teacher of psychology. I learned to trust him and came out to him as bi long before I was ready to tell other faculty.

Another new recruit, Dale Gilsdorf, was a tall, lanky man with untamed light brown hair. Dale exemplified the "new male" that I imagined would emerge in the coming decades. He was strongly influenced by the feminist movement and took the primary parenting role with his two daughters – a rare commitment for a man in those days. When his wife, also a professor, was offered an even more prestigious professorship on the east coast, they decided the children should live with him.

Dale, like me, had gone through a long and complex process of integrating his psychological understanding, his modern worldview, and his deep spirituality. We spent many leisurely walks together and occasional evenings in Dale's home discussing these issues. We also shared an interest in Eastern religions and meditation, although Dale was considerably more disciplined and experienced than I. That first year we team-taught a course together. We became close enough that I thought of him as an adopted brother. Our relationship proved to be one of the most healing and enhancing relationships in my life.

I got up the courage to ask him if he ever was sexually attracted to men. He responded with his gentle voice, "Dave, I love you, but I can't love you that way. I'm totally straight." It was a relief to have this out in the open, and wonderful that this interchange in no way distanced us from each other.

I don't believe I've ever had a straight man so completely understand that my wish for union with him was a message of love, not an attempt to seduce him. I was grateful for his love and only mildly disappointed. I find it more deeply fulfilling to be loved, and to be known and responded to honestly, than to have my immediate sexual wishes fulfilled.

Dale's intense interest in Eastern meditation and philosophy led him to move with his daughters to Ojai, California, where the Hindu writer Jiddu Krishnamurti had founded a school within a transformative meditating community. Dale and I remained close friends; Melissa and I regularly visited him and his daughters on the West coast.

Dale was not my only spiritual mentor. I attended a number of gatherings led by the poet Robert Bly. [5] There were some important weaknesses in Bly's work (and especially in his most popular book *Iron John*). Some of his views on male development were at odds with research; some were traditionally sexist. But Bly and other leaders of the mythopoetic men's movement recognized the importance of felt experience in the process of change for men. The academic writings of many in the pro-feminist men's movement failed to reach the souls of men who longed for change in themselves.

For more than a decade I alternated between the Men and Masculinity Conferences of pro-feminist men, where political correctness and social science dominated, and Bly's "Great Mother, New Father" gatherings, which I found inspiring. I became open about my own bisexuality at these conferences, and did not feel put down by Bly or by the participants. Many in the men's movement have moved beyond their initial defensive response to the women's and LBGTQ movements.

During gay liberation, gay men struggled with the lack of models for intimate male-to-male relationships. Bly pointed out that this lack of emotional intimacy among men has harmed straight men as well (Bly, 1990). But young men need more than older models; they need males who honor the females around them and the feminine within themselves. Traditional Western religions have been ambivalent about this. On the one hand, conservative religion in particular can be a "haven of patriarchal attitudes and masculine biases" (Elkins, 1998 p.109; Ault, 2004).

On the other hand, as David Elkins, a minister turned psychologist, wrote in his early book on spirituality without religious dogma," [6]

"My conservative church was one of the few places I could hear adults talk openly about love, kindness, and forgiveness.... Even crusty old farmers sometimes found the courage to express their gentler emotions at church. And the worship services, with their music, prayers and sermons, were often nourishing to the soul. So in this sense feminine values were honored, and both men and women were encouraged to nurture and develop their souls." (Elkins, 1998)

~ ~ ~

As one of the founding faculty of Governors State University, Dr. David Crispin strongly believed in experiential teaching. He had been on a sabbatical in Mexico when I began teaching at GSU in the fall of 1975. My previous jogging partner had left, so with Dave's return from Mexico, he and I began jogging together in the forest preserve once a week.

I enjoyed observing his classes and learning from him. He loved to teach, and occasionally did so when no student was in sight! Sometimes I would stop him, saying, "Dave, I don't feel like listening to a lecture right now," and that would be enough. He'd glance at me from the corner of his eyes, flash his impish but embarrassed smile, and shift gears – and we'd continue jogging or talking and enjoying being together.

Our weekly meetings provided a safe place for me to share my increasing involvement in the gay world. This was a world that Dave only knew of remotely; never before had one of his friends come out to him as gay or bi. But he remained non-judgmental, even when my life events surprised him. His loyal friendship over many years and his ability to help me explore the possible consequences of the decisions I was making led to my sharing more of my other life with him than with any other straight friend in that period. Since Melissa had asked me not to tell her any details of my gay involvements unless she asked specific questions, it helped me to discuss these with Dave.

When I became restless to be open with the faculty about being bisexual, Dave urged me not to come out until I had received tenure.

"Some of the administration might be prejudiced against gays," he reasoned, "and if they know you're bisexual, they may not evaluate your performance objectively."

With his encouragement, I discussed the issue with Associate Dean Bill Katz, a man of deep integrity. Bill echoed Dave's cautions. I followed their advice.

I liked doing scientific research and felt it would help my move toward early tenure if I published some quantitative research papers in reputable psychological journals. I needed help with data analysis and asked Ken Webber, a doctoral student at the University of Illinois. Ken was grateful for a chance to earn some extra money. He also liked to talk about family dynamics with me and to share difficulties he had had with his father. I sensed that in some ways he was looking up to me as a substitute father figure, even though I was only about ten years older than he was.

Several years later I contacted him again, this time about some research I was doing with bisexual married men. He suggested I bring the data to him in Champaign and he'd run it for me. By then the previous research he'd analyzed had been published and I was tenured. He had married and had completed his PhD. He was now licensed as a psychologist and was employed at U of I on a research team. We needed to spend a number of hours together working with the data, so he suggested I stay overnight with him. I looked forward to meeting his wife and celebrating his becoming a colleague.

When I arrived at his home, he explained that his wife was out of town. Ken and I went out for lunch. Cautiously he shared with me that he was currently in a men's group and found himself interested and aroused by one of the other men. He had begun to think he might be bisexual. He quizzed me about the subject, and I confirmed his suspicion that I was bisexual as well. He was curious about how Melissa handled this, and after some more dialogue

Ken indicated that he wanted to have a sexual experience with me.

I remembered my first gay sex with Franz in Cleveland. *I hope I can provide as positive an experience for Ken as Franz did for me,* I thought.

I left it to Ken to decide how much he wanted to explore and what he wanted to do. His first response was "Will you just hold me, and hug me?" As he lay down on the bed, and I hugged him, he seemed passive and childlike. But as he felt my caring, he became more active. I gently caressed his face, trying to sense his responses and move carefully and gently, slowing down or backing off if I felt any tensing or distancing. At first he mirrored my actions, caressing my face in return. But as he relaxed and became more trusting, he began to undress me. He became aroused.

After we both had climaxed, I continued to hold him in silence, our eyes closed. At some point I rose up on one elbow and gazed at his face. He seemed content and relaxed, but when he opened his eyes he looked a little startled to see me gazing at him. "How are you feeling?" I asked quietly.

"I'm okay," he said. "Thank you, Dave." Then he seemed to draw back into himself. Shortly after that we said goodnight and went to separate bedrooms.

I visited Ken's home four or five times over the next decade and got acquainted with his wife and two young children. Two or three times Ken arranged things so he and I would be alone, and we had sex together. Ken seemed to grow increasingly comfortable with this relationship.

After some years had passed, I was again planning a trip that took me through Champaign-Urbana. I phoned Ken to check about stopping by to see them. He responded, "I don't want our relationship to be sexual anymore, Dave. But you are welcome to come."

It seemed to me that we made the transition back to being friends and colleagues fairly easily. Ken's wife was at home for all of these visits; I'd been accepted as a guest of the family. Some years later I again phoned Ken. I was planning another trip through Champaign, and perhaps I could stop by their home. Ken's response was sharp and angry:

"I never want to see you again! Every time I see you, I feel like I'm being seduced and that you're expecting a sexual relationship with me!"

I was shocked. His anger seemed out of step with the way he'd welcomed me on my last several visits. Apparently my being bisexual had more potency for him than my wanting to continue the friendship. I felt bad that he could not trust me. Sadly, after several decades of friendship, the relationship had to end.

I still believe it is possible to retain friendships through major changes in the individuals' roles (for example, from teacher-student to peer or from sexual to non-sexual, or the reverse).

For example, there was Ted. Our relationship began as professor and student, although we were close in age. About a decade after Ted's graduation from a master's program in which I taught, we decided to drive together to one of the annual "Men and Masculinity" conferences. On the road trip, he shared with me that he, also, was a bisexual married man.

Ted was a talented organist and loved classical music. We sometimes attended concerts together. For a period, our friendship occasionally included sex together. One time, Ted had stopped at my house to pick me up and ride into Chicago together for an afternoon organ concert at Rockefeller Chapel. When I got home later, Nathan asked me, "Is Ted gay?"

"Nathan, it's good that you're curious and I'm glad you feel free to ask me," I replied. "But I don't have the right to tell you whether someone is gay or not. Everyone has to decide for themselves who they want to tell about their own sexuality."

After a year or so, our relationship turned back into friendship. We remained good friends for many years after that. When I learned he was dying of cancer, I drove many miles to visit him in the hospital.

~ ~ ~

Workshops I attended on family therapy and the variety of relationships I developed with colleagues, mentors, and adult peers helped to heal the wounds from my adolescence. I also began to look again at my parents. I realized that I had not had as close a relationship with Dad as I might have wished. When we kids got up in the morning, Mom served us breakfast and helped us get ready for school. Dad was still sleeping because he had worked the late afternoon/evening shift. When weekends came, he often had projects to do. He missed farming and spent a lot of time plowing, seeding, and caring for vegetable gardens. In addition, he served in leadership positions at the Methodist church, where he frequently functioned as the janitor and fix-it man. Mom once confronted him with her frustration that, when he was off work, he did not spend enough time at home.[7]

I didn't confront my feelings about the fact that Dad had been absent during much of my childhood until Melissa and I had become parents ourselves. I made a conscious commitment to play a more equal role with Melissa in parenting.

My mom and dad, now retired, spent winters in an RV camp near Tampa, and our kids were about six when the four of us drove down to be with my parents during part of Christmas break. Dad had suffered some minor strokes but had recovered sufficiently that he could walk around normally.

At one point I went for a walk alone with Dad. I tried to make this an occasion of sharing and not of blame as I expressed to Dad that I felt disappointed that he and I had spent so little time together. Dad immediately teared up and responded, "I loved you, David. I loved all you kids. But I couldn't find any way to keep us all fed and clothed if I didn't work the shift that paid the highest wages."

It was clear that he had made the best decision he could given the circumstances, and that it had nothing to do with his not caring about us or about me in particular. I was grateful that I had shared my criticism and not let myself continue to wonder about the reasons for his behavior. It was only three or four months later, in March of 1977, that Dad died.

As for Mom, I gradually realized that my view of her was unrealistically idealized. She wasn't the perfect mother I liked to imagine. Apparently she was a better mother to me than she was to my sisters, at least partly because of the narrow gender roles expected for girls in those days. But I came to understand that Mom had given up her life's dream of being a religious education director in order to raise us five children. Despite Mom's and Dad's limitations, as I look back I am tremendously grateful for the many ways each of them showed love, for the incredible sacrifices they made. I deeply appreciate the way they accepted each of us as individuals and did not compare us or expect us to follow the same pattern.

CHAPTER 13
EXPLORING THE GAY COMMUNITY

Living in a large metropolis like Chicago meant that, for the first time in my life, I had access to a variety of social services geared specifically to bisexuals. A journal entry I wrote in 1977 reads:

> "This was the year I found my body...
>   in dance and in swimming –
>   finally learning to push it;
>   in bed, learning to enjoy sex –
>   in and out of love;
>   and getting to know (my body's) limits."

Gradually I learned the codes and mores of three different venues for connecting with gay and bisexual men: the bars, the baths, and the "wanted" ads in gay newspapers. I lived in the exurbs, far from the gay scene of Chicago, so there was very little chance of my meeting other gay or bi men in my own area. Not that they don't exist, but with very few exceptions most suburban gay men and almost all suburban bisexual men are closeted.

In bars or baths I met up with a number of likeable and caring gay men. Most of my encounters with them were limited to one, two, or three meetings. My real wish was for both a deep friendship and a sexual relationship with a man. Although I was not conscious of it at the time, a big part of me was longing for a man I could love. And I was "looking for love in all the wrong places." Eventually I gave up the bar and bath scenes. But I don't regret that I started there. Like the early explorers of America, I learned that my maps were wrong. But I also learned that there are exciting and valuable aspects of the new territory I was exploring.

For much of American history, gay bars and baths were the only public spaces where it was safe to be out. In Chicago in the late 1970s there was very little risk of the police raiding the bars. [8] Men's baths, going back at least to ancient Greece and Rome, are places where men can be comfortable in the nude together. There is a sort of communal acceptance of the body without some of the inhibitions and pressures of dressing right and displaying one's class and social status. And in gay baths there is freedom to be in couples, threesomes, or groups. I found this incredibly liberating; it was radically different from the inhibited view of sex that prevailed in the 1950s in the small town I grew up in.

So I benefited from the bath and bar experiences. They sometimes satisfied my lust for men, and they freed me from some of my sexual inhibitions. They also helped me realize that casual sex, even in its extreme form of anonymous sex in baths, does not have to be impersonal. Just because one has only known a person for a short time does not mean that the interaction is without respect or caring. Sometimes a very limited relationship can be quite intimate, tender, or wonderfully playful. I began to question the idea that sex belongs only in long-lasting relationships and that short encounters are not valuable.

But as I became clearer about my longings, I increasingly focused on ads in the gay newspapers. From the late 1970s right up till about 2000, I met most of the men I dated through these. I looked for phrases such as "seeking a real friendship, and more if it develops." A series of partners ensued.

The first continuing relationship I recall was with a man about my age who was an aesthete like me. Edward was a professional architect who lived in a stunningly beautiful apartment overlooking Lake Michigan in a far north section of Chicago. His prematurely white hair fit the monochrome décor of his condo, furnished in chrome, glass, and black leather. He was bright, cool, and pleasant to be with, although eventually I felt he was overly intellectual. I missed the kind of emotional warmth I longed for in a sexual partner.

I don't recall how I first met Fred – probably through an ad he placed in one of Chicago's gay papers. He was about 5'9", slightly shorter than me, and had thick graying hair which made him look a bit older than me, although in fact we were both in our forties. As was my pattern, we met in a safe public space where I could get a sense of his personality before I risked going to his home or inviting him to mine. On a later date, I did go to Fred's condo.

After offering me some wine, Fred showed me around. He had a massage table set up in one room; although he hadn't mentioned it before, he was a professional massage therapist. After some comfortable talk, he offered to give me a massage. Soon I was very relaxed. He asked if I would enjoy a genital massage. I consented, and he focused his attention completely on pleasing me. Slowly and gently he brought me to a climax; then he wrapped me in a warm terrycloth robe. His relaxed and unassuming style helped me to really enjoy our time together. We said goodbye with a warm hug and looked forward to our next date.

We attended several operas together; Fred chose them, since he knew much more about opera than I. We met a number of times, usually for dinner, followed by going to his home and having sex together. But gradually our relationship cooled off. It's hard to describe just why.

We ended our dating relationship as friends. We occasionally ran into each other at intermission at the opera house and chatted. I appreciated Fred's gentleness and warmth, but eventually I wasn't interested in resuming the dating relationship. As far as I know, there were no areas of conflict between us, but there also did not seem to be much spark.

~ ~ ~

Although I'd negotiated exactly what I thought I wanted at Governors State University, after two or three years of teaching both academic psychology and the practice of counseling, I missed seeing clients myself. I feared becoming too theoretical. When I'm actually working directly with clients, I recognize the limitations of the theories that I use.

Professors at GSU were encouraged to spend one day a week doing work in the community. I decided to devote some of those hours to providing counseling services on a sliding payment scale. Seven counselors formed a private service, with Bill Rogge and me supervising the other counselors as well as seeing clients, and with Susan Summers and Mary Jahn (two graduates of our master's program) and Melissa (with her master's in psychiatric nursing) as counselors.

In a nearby bank, we found a two-room office that we could rent together. I furnished one room with a couch that opened up and could be used as a bed. I was already open about my gay relationships with all of the counselors in our service.

The couch that opened up into a bed soon had a frequent visitor named Patrick. I first met Patrick through an ad in one of Chicago's gay newspapers. He was also bisexual, married, and a professor in a college in the area. We developed an extended relationship, meeting once every two or three weeks over the next couple of years in the private space of the office.

Patrick was open with his wife about being bisexual. They both were devout Catholics, but they accepted his bisexuality. His wife and I had been active in the peace movement and had participated in some demonstrations together. The fact that she had met me seemed to make my relationship with Patrick more comfortable for her. At the time, that would *not* have been the case for Melissa.

Both Patrick and I had many other commitments, so our meetings weren't frequent. But both of us felt good about being steadily involved with someone, rather than cruising in gay spots or placing ads in the "men seeking men" sections of the papers. Patrick was a few years older than I and bigger in every way. He was about five inches taller, and although he was not fat, he must have weighed a bit over 210 pounds compared to my 175. Both of us had religious and spiritual interests, and sexually we were very compatible.

Our relationship was pleasant and respectful, but eventually it became a bit routine. I came to suspect that his Irish Catholicism had left him emotionally suppressed. I respected that he had tried to work through his own personal stance on religion and that he was involved in leading others in rituals and workshops that were inclusive, rather than assuming that everyone should embrace his own Catholic beliefs. Yet after a year or so I found myself somewhat bored with our conversations. Often I experienced him as emotionally flat. It was hard to put my finger on what was missing, but by this point in my gay life I wanted not just sex but intimacy with my primary gay partner. I believe Patrick was being authentic and sharing what he could, but I just wasn't getting the kind of emotional closeness I was looking for. Fortunately for us both, a new relationship closer to his work developed for him, so when I suggested that we meet less frequently, it fit his needs as well.

We continued to correspond occasionally, but a few years later I was surprised to get a phone call from his wife. For a wife to knowingly call her husband's sexual partner must have taken courage. She told me that Patrick had died of cancer. I was extremely grateful to her for having the compassion and generosity to let me know.

~ ~ ~

After a couple years of getting to know the LBGT community, I wanted to contribute. I offered to lead a group for married bisexual men under the auspices of Gay Horizons, Chicago's major LBGT organization.

Allen was one of eight bisexual married men who were in the men's support group. One of my personal principles is that important information that impacts a significant relationship should be shared with the other person in that relationship, who in Allen's case was his wife. So when Allen disclosed to the group that he was having a relationship with another man, I was uneasy that he wasn't telling the truth to his wife, who he claimed was his closest friend. As counselor and group leader, it was important that I not encourage shame around genuine identity issues. I was sure Allen would recognize that my addressing the issue of infidelity was not a criticism of his need for gay involvements.

I decided to question his decision not to tell his wife, taking a gentle approach. In front of the group, I shared my own experience: "Whenever I am dishonest on an important issue, it affects both my partner and me. Any dishonesty builds a barrier between Melissa and me. Melissa trusts that I will never deceive her. If I hide an important aspect of my life, I believe that she experiences the silence as a barrier. It weakens the trust. So I've come to a decision not to keep secrets, even if working through the issue is painful or frightening."

My disclosure deeply affected Allen. He told us that he longed to be more open with his wife and that he had tried to share some of his feelings toward men with her, but that doing so had scared her and pushed her away. She had warned him not to say anything more. As I later realized in my research with such marriages, the wife is often complicit in the husband's decision to keep his gay life a secret.

Allen said he wished he and his wife could be open on very difficult issues, but it seemed that there was a wall between them no matter how he handled it, honestly or dishonestly, so he chose not to risk losing her altogether. From his perspective, he loved her too much to insist on absolute integrity for himself.

In future sessions, Allen reassessed his part in the secrecy. He questioned whether he might be underestimating his wife's ability to deal with the issue of his bisexuality. But he didn't reconsider the moral issue itself, his own honesty versus his holding onto the relationship. In his own perception of the dilemma, nothing had changed.

What changed in me was that I developed a new respect for differences. I became more humble about my rules for intimate relationships; perhaps they don't apply to every couple. I respected that Allen was unable to see a way to live out his relationship without some barrier between him and his wife. I feel it is amazing and fortunate that I have a wife who has become secure enough in her own worth that she can accept my being actively bisexual, yet not feel she has to give up her own integrity.

~ ~ ~

Although at this stage I was selective about whom I came out to regarding my sexual orientation, my interest in gender issues was widely known. In 1983 I became one of the founding members of NOMAS, a new national men's group to parallel the very effective work of the National Organization for Women (NOW). As we planned "Men and Masculinity" conferences, straight, gay, and bisexual men worked together and got to know each other as individuals. We began to recognize that it was in our own interest to challenge the narrow gender roles that prevented many men from experiencing emotional intimacy with other men. These roles not only fed men's violence against women, but also their violence against other men.

We also worked hard to blend the best of men's and women's styles of communication – to overcome the competitive and aggressive aspects of traditional masculinity. These pro-feminist men became a wonderfully accepting community for the emergence of my bisexuality. The group provided the rare context in which straight men affirmed my gay side and gay men affirmed my straight side. Soon other men in the organization came out as bisexual as well.

After three years of living in the Chicago area, I had moved into a pattern of fairly steady gay relationships. I was interested in expanding my knowledge of other married bisexual men, to learn the various ways they managed their lives with their wives and families and their participation in gay culture and male partnerships. It was about this time that I received tenure at Governors State University, which made it safer for me to be open about my bisexuality. I told my department colleagues that I was bisexual and that I wanted to do research on mixed orientation couples in which the husband is gay or bi and the wife is heterosexual.

In addition to the group I led, there were two other groups of bisexual men in the Chicago suburbs. Their members, plus an ad in Chicago's gay newspaper, yielded a sample of thirty husbands. I requested that each husband in an acknowledged couple (in which the wife knew about her husband's bisexuality) ask his wife if she was willing to be interviewed by Melissa. Eleven wives consented.

Our research had unexpected benefits for Melissa and me. Interviewing the wives gave Melissa a chance to meet other women who were dealing with their husbands' bisexuality, providing clear evidence that she was not alone. It also provided confirmation that our communication and our emotional sharing were better than many of the couples in the study – partly, of course, because our professions involved ample training and practice in effective communication.

The details of our study of mixed-orientation marriages have been published elsewhere, but here is what we found: the husbands who had disclosed their bisexuality before the marriage or had been open with their wives once they began to have male partners developed more trust in their marital relationships. They were able to work out agreements that let them continue both their gay involvements and their marriages. When I called the husbands two years later and again seven years later, most of these acknowledged couples were still together, and the husbands were satisfied with their marriages.

The husbands in secretive marriages were not as satisfied. They often felt guilty about their secret lives and did not have deep emotional communication with their wives. Nonetheless, the percentage of secretive couples still together seven years later was just as high as in that of the acknowledged group: 67% were still together in the final follow-up.

In the secretive couples who broke up, the split tended to happen when the wife realized that her husband had been cheating. Couples in the acknowledged marriages tended to break up when the wife had developed a relationship with a man other than her husband and found this new relationship more satisfying. However, other wives in the continuing marriages also experimented with romantic/sexual relationships with other men but eventually chose to remain with their bisexual husbands.

Many of the wives who had been in secretive marriages at the time of the initial interview were moving toward more open acknowledgement of the husbands' bisexual behavior by the last interview.

Some therapists and clergy have counseled bisexual husbands to give up all gay involvements. The belief that bisexual husbands who had experienced gay sex for a period would then give it up was, for the most part, disproved. Our sample included seven husbands who resolved to cease all homosexual activity. In the final follow-up, 86% of these men (all but one) admitted that they had not lived out their resolve. The one man who succeeded did so because of a combination of deep love for his wife and very strong religious beliefs that extramarital sex was wrong.

The research interviews benefitted me in two ways. I understood more clearly that for this type of marriage to work, the husband must treat the relationship with the wife as primary; the gay relationship is rarely sustainable unless the gay partner honors that the heterosexual marriage must come first. I was uncomfortable with this discovery – my fantasy was that the two partnerships should be equal. But the research strongly suggested that, at least in the early phase of open relationships, wives needed to feel that their husbands' relationship with them was primary. They also needed clear boundaries and their own separate life and support system. These conditions were true in the research sample, and they were true in my personal experience with Melissa.

An interesting coping pattern emerged among many of the husbands: they handled the primacy issue by totally separating friendships with men and sexual relationships with men. As one of the husbands phrased it, "I have men friends and I have 'fucking buddies,' and I never mix them." It was as if, were they to have both a friendship *and* a sexual relationship with the same man, it would feel too much like the marriage relationship.

But this strategy was completely at odds with my own desires and personal values. I longed for sexual and emotional intimacy with both my current male partner and my wife. In this respect, our marriage and the way I live my bisexuality seem to be rather rare.

In my early analysis of the results, following the three-year interviews, the men in the open relationships appeared to have deeper personal integration. Deceit could destroy the trust that was so essential for an open relationship to work.

However, the follow-up interviews revealed that the decision for a secretive relationship was not simply the husbands' choice: the wife often participated in keeping it a secret, as Allen's wife had. The study results made me even more aware of how rare it was for wives to develop the courage and strength to face their husband's bisexuality, as my wife had. The fact that there were some aspects that Melissa did not want to know about seemed more understandable and easier to respect.

~ ~ ~

Although Melissa and I benefitted from doing this research together, this period brought the most difficult and sustained emotional struggle we ever experienced in our lives together. At one point, Melissa decided she needed some time away from me, to get clear in her own mind about whether she wanted to continue our marriage or end it.

Fortunately, Melissa had a trusting platonic friendship with Bill Rogge, the GSU professor who had first interviewed me and urged me join the faculty there. Bill and his wife had separated several years before, and he was now in a serious relationship with another woman but did not live with her. Melissa asked Bill if she could move in for several weeks to get more perspective on our marriage. All three of us were comfortable with this arrangement, although I was very anxious about whether Melissa might decide to leave me permanently. I worried, *Am I really going to lose her? I love her so much. Yet, I don't think I can be myself and deny my bisexuality.*

The trust among us and the fact that Bill lived only a few miles away made it possible to manage this respite while still parenting our kids. I don't remember how long it took; Melissa thinks it was six weeks. Finally she called me, asking that we get together so she could tell me her decision. "Can I come home tonight, after the kids are in bed?" she asked.

"Of course, I want you to come."

What a relief when she walked in the door with her suitcase in hand! "I'm ready to stay. It's hard, but I want to be with you." We both broke down in tears. We hugged each other – a long caring hug. When I regained enough composure, I assured her, "I love you. I'm so glad you're back. I will do what I can to make sure you *know* that I love you. Thank God you're back. I am so lucky!"

CHAPTER 14
PAUL AND NICK

Perhaps the most surprising date I ever had was my second one with Paul, a gay man I met through a "men seeking men" ad I had posted. Following my usual pattern, our first face-to-face meeting was in a restaurant; Paul was a short, attractive man around my age, and I enjoyed conversing with him.

A week or two later Paul called me and invited me to come to his home. He lived a good hour and a half from me, but his directions were clear, and I arrived at the agreed-upon time in mid-afternoon. Our plan was to have alone time together and then go out to eat. When I arrived at his home, I noticed that bushes over six feet high shielded his front door from the street. I rang the bell, and this attractive man opened the door and said smilingly, "Hi Dave! Welcome to my house." He was standing there totally nude.

We both laughed in delight. I marveled at his courage and enjoyed his being so comfortable. I gave him a big hug and stripped off my own clothes – inside the house. We had some pleasant conversation and some playful sex. He was easy to converse with, as well as fun to be with sexually.

Unfortunately, given the distance between our homes and the fact that we both had busy professional schedules, it didn't seem realistic to continue the relationship. I was realizing that it might take a long search before my longing for a male sexual relationship that included deep friendship would be fulfilled.

I began to look for gay or bi partners at personal growth workshops. Of course, most of the men attending workshops were straight. But it's safe in that setting to suggest going out for a meal or a drink. There are subtle ways to check out another man's orientation, such as listing three places we might go, with one of them a gay bar. If he chooses the gay bar, I might ask, "Are you familiar with that place?" If he says "Yes," I'm at least fairly sure he's not homophobic.

I met Nick in one of these workshops. He was not afraid to show his vulnerability as he described an interpersonal conflict in his life. Something he said gave me a clue that he was interested in art. So when the workshop ended, I asked him if he'd like to meet sometime at the Art Institute of Chicago for lunch.

We went there several times during our brief relationship. On our second or third date, we were waiting to cross Michigan Avenue to enter the museum. It was a beautiful sunny day, and a cluster of other pedestrians stood near us. The weather, our mutual love of art, the grandeur of Chicago's architecture, and of course our attraction to each other all conspired to make us bubbly and childlike. The light changed to green, and spontaneously both Nick and I began skipping across the street like school kids! Our delight in each other erased all thought of worrying about what others might think.

Another time, Nick invited me back to his apartment. He served us each a glass of iced herb tea at his kitchen table, and we chatted and relaxed for a while. Then he surprised me by asking, "Would you enjoy taking a bath?"

"You know, that sounds great," I responded. It was a hot and humid day, and I could feel the dust of the city sticking to my sweaty body.

He left me in the kitchen, and I could hear him running the water in the bathroom. When he came back, he asked me to close my eyes.

"I want to lead you to the tub and undress you. I want

you simply to concentrate on all your senses, except your sight."

In the bathroom, he gently unbuttoned my clothes. I felt the warmth of his hands and smelled the scented bath oil in the moist air. He guided me into the tub; I felt trusting and comfortable. At first he used a soft, hot washcloth to bathe my whole body as I sat in the tub. Then he had me lean a bit forward, and he stroked my back with a wet but slightly abrasive sponge. When I stepped out of the tub, still with my eyes closed, still trusting, he toweled me off gently. Then he led me into his bedroom, and had me lie down on the bed. I was feeling clean, relaxed, and comfortable being nude before him.

"I just want you to continue to let me please you," he stated. He hugged me. I asked, "Don't you want anything?"

"No," he responded, "this is just for you to enjoy." Slowly and lovingly he caressed me and rubbed my whole body with oils. Then he messaged my genitals until I reached orgasm. The whole experience was so nurturing, so deeply satisfying.

When our date was over, I assumed we'd see each other again. I wondered if I would be able to please him as much as he had pleased me. But we never dated again. I don't know why, but it seems that he chose to give me this wonderful day, but not to continue the relationship.

I think that Nick was much more experienced in gay life than I. Perhaps he saw this as a kind of initiation into the deeper sensuality of gay male experience. Whatever his motives, I'm grateful for his gentle gift.

After a series of relatively short relationships, my dream of a long-lasting, deep friendship with a gay sexual partner began to fade. Since I had a very satisfying marriage, as well as a deep investment in raising our two children, for the most part my need for emotional intimacy was being met in my marriage and family. I enjoyed the process of dating and had enough sexual and interpersonal satisfaction that I did not focus obsessively on finding a permanent gay partner.

CHAPTER 15
COMING OUT TO FAMILY

I was changing from viewing myself as heterosexual to realizing that I was bisexual and that my gay desires were not going to fade away. I began to want to be open about it with my family.

Melissa and I had lived in the Chicago area less than two years when my father died on May 4, 1977. He had already had some heart ailments and one serious stroke, so his death was not unexpected, but it came suddenly, with no hospitalization first. At the burial, I knelt down beside the grave, picked up some loose soil, tossed it onto the casket, and began sobbing deeply. Greg was standing beside me. He put his hand on my shoulder and asked, "Are you okay?" At the time, I thought I was just expressing my grief. But years later I realized that, although the grief was genuine, I also was feeling relief. For reasons that are not entirely clear to me, the death of my father freed me to be open about my bisexuality. Perhaps because his family had been so puritan and repressive of sexuality, his death became a symbol of the end of my repression.

I still wonder, *How would Dad have reacted if I had told him I was bisexual?* I don't believe he would have rejected me, yet somehow I had intuited that I should delay coming out to my family until after his death.

Less than six months later, I told my mother about my bisexuality. She was still living in the small town in which we five children were raised and was still active in the local Methodist church. But she had always opposed racial discrimination and had a strong sense of social justice, so I expected her to be supportive. I also thought she'd be concerned about my marriage to Melissa.

She didn't understand why it's important for gays to come out. She told me she was disgusted by displays of affection between gay men that she'd seen in the media. (Like many heterosexuals, she wasn't conscious of the double standard, forgetting that it's common for heterosexual couples to kiss and have other displays of affection in public.)

But the gay issue was clearly secondary to my open marriage with Melissa, whom Mom had come to love as one of her daughters. Mom said that every man she had known who got involved in extramarital sex had ruined his marriage, and she feared this would happen to Melissa and me. I never thought she would reject me, and she never did. But I think now that it was insensitive of me to come out so soon after Dad's death.

I don't know how deep my mother's struggle was as she grappled with my uncommon marriage and with bisexuality, a topic that was so hidden at that time that even the gay world was only beginning to acknowledge it. [9] She did talk about her concerns about what would be best for me in the long run. And she repeatedly emphasized her love for both Melissa and me. Later that year when I attended a huge gay rights march in Washington DC, I wrote her about the joy and hope I'd felt in meeting others working for gay liberation. I tried to help her connect it to the marches for the liberation of India that she had identified with, led by her hero Gandhi.

My younger sister Carol and I have so much in common that it was easiest to come out to her first among my siblings. Like me, she is a social activist. She was ordained in the United Methodist Church, and her first parish was very close to Greenwich Village, the gay area in New York City. The minister of the Methodist parish in the Village, the Rev. Paul Abels, became her friend and mentor during the first years of her ministry. He was gay and was in a committed relationship with another gay man. At that time the United Methodist denomination had not developed a clear policy concerning openly gay ministers. Paul came out publicly in a November 1977 article in the *New York Times* describing covenant services he was conducting for gay couples. I told Carol that I really wanted to meet Paul when I came to New York City to visit her and her husband Monty. Carol had become an ally of lesbians and gays, believing that the Christian church should be inclusive, so I had no fears regarding her attitude toward gays. But I didn't know how she would feel about my being a married bisexual.

In New York, Carol, Monty, and I went out for a meal with Paul. I enjoyed the discussion and let Paul know that I supported his decision to be open about his ministry and his sexual orientation. Later, when I returned with Carol and Monty to their apartment, I shifted the subject to myself.

"I really appreciated meeting Paul, and I know you two have been supportive of his continuing his ministry and his being open about being gay. Now I want to be open with you. Like Paul, I have realized gradually that I am sexually attracted to men."

As I shared this, looking directly at them, I did not see anything in their faces that suggested they were shocked; I knew they were going to be supportive.

Carol said, "Whatever is going on, Dave, you know I love you, and I will always love you."

"That means a lot to me," I responded. As I later wrote in my journal, I was surprised by how much Carol's acceptance mattered to me.

"But unlike Paul," I continued, "I'm not gay. I'm bisexual. Melissa has known about my attraction to men for over ten years now, although it's only in the last three years that I've become active in the gay community."

"So how are you planning to deal with it?" Carol asked.

"I love Melissa very much, and I have no intention of leaving her. But I feel that I have to explore my gay side as well."

I could tell that this part of the conversation was harder for both Carol and Monty. Nonetheless, when I flew back to Chicago, my strongest feeling was "they still love me." I was grateful for their support.

We continued to discuss the issue in letters back and forth. Weeks after my visit Carol wrote, "Monty and I were glad you felt support when you were with us. I'm still very upset about what's going on with you. It would be easier for me to deal with your being gay (or bisexual) if you simply had said 'I've discovered I'm gay and I don't feel I can now live with Melissa,' and if you were talking about trying to develop a deep and meaningful relationship with a man (or even another woman)."

Carol opposed sex that isn't part of a commitment of love; she also believed that open marriages rarely worked. She predicted that Melissa and I would eventually divorce if I continued on this path. She closed by writing, "It's hard to condense this mix of emotions to a few pages. Please read it with love between the lines."

Both Carol and Monty have continued to talk with me about the church and homosexuality. They have been direct about their fears for my marriage with Melissa, but in a letter she wrote about three years after our meeting in New York, Carol had softened about my continuing involvement in gay life. She and Monty have remained allies in the struggle for gay rights.

Carol sometimes teases me, pointing out that because I am a married bisexual, "You are not exactly the best poster boy for gay rights issues when it comes to confronting the church!" She is well aware that the church has an easier time embracing gay relationships that conform to the model of heterosexual, monogamous marriage. Embracing bisexuality and the concept of open marriage is a much bigger stretch for many Christians, not just for Carol.

~ ~ ~

Heterosexual marriage in contemporary culture is viewed as moral only if it is monogamous. Of course, the Hebrew Scriptures condoned men's having several wives and concubines if they could afford it. But most critics of gay relationships are unaware of the many ways the concept of marriage has changed over the centuries. [10]

If one thinks about it, it is absurd to expect the relationship between two men (or two women) to mirror the relationship between a man and a woman, given that the culture's expectations for men and women are so different.

Men have traditionally been taught to initiate sex; women have been taught to set limits on sex. Obviously, when pregnancy and parenthood is a possible outcome of sexual behavior, the number of sexual partners and the frequency of sexual interaction have practical implications. So it is understandable that women have been socialized to set these limits. In gay male sexual interactions, being lax about the limits has fewer negative consequences than in heterosexual interactions.

Predictably, studies of committed gay male couples show that they often accept that their partner can have sex outside their relationship, so long as it is does not threaten their own health or love commitment. In short, many gay marriages are open marriages, and unless major changes occur in the way men are socialized, this is likely to continue to be the case for male couples.

~ ~ ~

My sister Lucille and her husband John had some

discussions about open marriage in the early 1970's. I came out to her more fully, discussing my bisexuality shortly after coming out to Carol and Monty. By then Lucille had been divorced for a number of years and was dating again. I couldn't predict how Lucille would feel about my coming out, but I trusted that she would not reject me and would work through any negative feelings she might have. In fact, after I came out, Lucille showed her deep caring for Melissa and me and respected that the situation was one we had to work out in our own way.

I visited Greg and told him that I had something important I wanted to share with him. He listened carefully as I explained about my bisexual life. He surprised me by wondering if he had played a role in my becoming gay, recalling times when he and his friends didn't want his little brother tagging along.

"Perhaps I failed to be a good model as older brother," he suggested.

I appreciated his concern but assured him that I doubted those events had any impact on my sexual orientation. I was well-read in the research on the causes of homosexuality and explained to Greg that there was no evidence of any consistent family dynamic that distinguished families with gay sons from those with straight. The discussion may not have been easy for Greg, but it did not create distance between us. His wife Monica tends to avoid discussing anything controversial, and when I've visited I've tried to respect this, so I don't know how she feels about my bisexuality. She has been a wonderful host on my visits.

Both Greg and Monica are active in the Methodist church. In 2012, decades after I'd come out to Greg, the Methodist annual conference was debating their ban on gay clergy. Greg stood up and said, "My brother served as a minister in a Methodist Church. If you vote in favor of this proposal, you are rejecting the ministry of my brother." Unfortunately, the homophobic rules were renewed. But Greg's courage in publicly disagreeing with the actions of his own denomination moved me. Clearly, he has accepted who I am.

During the same year that I came out to Greg, Melissa and I took a trip west, including a visit to Fort Collins where my youngest brother Len and his wife Jessica lived. I told Len I wanted to share something with him, but that he didn't need to respond to it immediately. He could take time to digest it.

At the end of our trip, I asked Len how my disclosure had affected our relationship. Len, who had always been a poor correspondent, said, "Well, Dave, I'll write to you as often as I ever have!"

After I'd come out to all my siblings, I asked my mother how she thought my Aunt Sylvia would react. Aunt Sylvia was my mother's closest sister, a wonderfully warm and loving person who was also a graduate of the very conservative Moody Bible Institute. Years before, when I had been on Oprah Winfrey's and Phil Donahue's shows [11] as a researcher and counselor for LBGTQs, Mom had arranged to watch with Aunt Sylvia. "I really admire your willingness to be helpful and caring to unfortunate people like that," my aunt commented. It didn't occur to her that I might be one of those "unfortunate people."

~ ~ ~

By the 1980s I had explored gay culture in Chicago and had had a number of relationships, none of them long-lasting. The Men and Masculinity conferences and my serving on the NOMAS Council often put me in the company of gay, straight, and bisexual men who respected and cared about me. One year our conference met in Seattle Washington, with the theme "Our Fathers, Our Children, Ourselves." On the second evening something in a small group meeting resurrected my strong emotional responses to Dad's death. I couldn't calm down, so I set out on a long walk. It was a warm evening, and our conference was on a small college campus in a safe area. I walked for over a mile. The exercise got me more in touch with my body, and I found myself crying, walking faster, and sobbing harder and harder. Eventually I headed down a street toward the men's dorm where we were staying. As rounded a corner, I saw a man standing in the shadows leaning against the building where we'd earlier enjoyed a folk music concert. It was Fred Small, one of the musicians. He walked toward me and said gently, "What's wrong, Dave?" as he opened his long arms and embraced me. He held me like a father should hold his crying son. For a while I couldn't stop crying, but Fred held me as if time was of no importance. I could feel that he would be there to hear me when I was ready. Finally I shared the pain I felt in relation to Dad. In those moments, Fred was my ideal dad – and it didn't matter so much what had happened years before.

What became clear, both from this encounter and from later men's meetings and groups, was that other men could provide what I needed in the present, whether or not I had received what I thought I needed from Dad in the past.

CHAPTER 16
COMING OUT BEYOND FAMILY

I knew a number of gay men who were rejected when they came out to their families. Yet I believe that it is important to be who you really are, and that you can choose who surrounds you. It is common in gay culture to speak of "my chosen family."

I recognized the possibility of isolation and even of martyrdom if I came out: Harvey Milk, the first openly gay person elected to office in California, had been assassinated only a few months before I was tenured. I slowed down my coming out process to avoid losing my job or my relationship with Melissa, Nathan, and Michelle. I gave the people around me more time to learn about men's sexuality and the gay world. I was teaching counseling students, most of whom wanted to understand and were open to accepting people who were different from themselves. I predicted that eventually our culture would become more accepting of the blurring of gender lines and more affirmative of sexuality in general and homosexuality in particular.

After I received tenure at GSU in 1979, I came out to my friends and colleagues. At department meetings, we had talked about my research on mixed-orientation marriages (MOMs), including bisexual men in heterosexual marriages. During one of these discussions, I came out personally. Everyone was polite, and the chair of the department, Dr. Addison Woodward, was very supportive, as were two of the women professors, Dr. Helen Hughes and Dr. Rachel Berg. My close friendships with straight males did not suffer.

But one male colleague in the counseling program, Dr.

Ken Weig, had a hard time with the gay part of my life. I had worked closely with him on a number of issues related to students and curricula. He was generally comfortable hugging men as well as women, and until my coming out, he had been comfortable hugging me. When I became open with colleagues about my bisexuality, he suddenly stopped touching me in any way. The change was very noticeable.

But gradually, as the months went by, he resumed the touch that came so naturally to him. Although it was never spoken about directly, I suspect it became clear to him that I was still the same person he had known before I came out.

For a number of years our psych and counseling department had a faculty member who was theologically conservative. He learned that I had been ordained and felt that we had a common interest in religion. At first he enjoyed discussing biblical material with me, but after I came out as bisexual to the faculty in my department, his feelings changed.

One day two students reported to me that this professor, in a classroom lecture, had described his theory that there is a place at the base of the brain where the devil can enter a person. He told the students that he now realized that one of his colleagues was homosexual, which meant that the devil had entered his brain stem. He indirectly identified me.

"What should we do about his teaching this nonsense and talking that way about you?" one of the students asked me.

"I'm grateful you've told me this," I assured the students, "but you don't need to do a thing."

When I told one of the administrators, he told me he had already heard similar reports and had been debating what action to take. "Since that professor is tenured, trying to dismiss him would require a legal battle," he said, obviously reluctant to pursue it.

I was frustrated about simply letting a professor get away with this behavior. But I told the administrator, "I think this professor's statements are so absurd that most of the students recognize them as products of his unbalanced mental state. Perhaps it isn't worth making a fuss about it."

Soon after this discussion an amusing coincidence occurred. This unstable faculty member had talked to me about the New Testament book of Revelation, declaring that the number 666 is a numeric symbol for the devil. When my next bill for renewing my membership in the American Counselor Association arrived, I noticed that my membership number ended in 666! But I didn't bother to tell my colleague.

A year or so after my coming out, most of my relationships with faculty in my department were back to what they had been before my disclosure. But things were different with some professors in other departments who didn't know me personally. A few years later, with increased awareness of the AIDS epidemic, my work assignments were revised to allow me to oversee HIV-AIDS prevention work throughout the University's various curricula. I reached out to all faculty members who taught courses in which this subject would be appropriate. Most of these faculty members seemed to appreciate my outreach; many encouraged me to speak to their classes or asked me for suggestions for incorporating information on prevention into their class material.

Occasionally I learned of faculty outside my field who found my involvement in HIV prevention and my concern for gay rights amusing. I had joined two faculty women in signing a letter to the editor of our campus newspaper that closed with, "Yours from three feminist faculty." Since I was part of the feminist men's movement, I was comfortable calling myself a feminist. Soon after that letter was printed, my graduate assistant, a gay man working with me on an AIDS-related research project, overheard some faculty from the Business College commenting about the letter. One professor had remarked, "That professor Matteson, he doesn't even know what sex he is!"

~ ~ ~

I'd been a member of the local Unitarian Universalist church for at least six years and was occasionally called upon to preach. As early as 1970, at the denomination's national level, there had been resolutions accepting people as members regardless of sexual orientation, although as yet there were no regulations regarding ordaining openly gay ministers. In one of my sermons, I came out to the local congregation. I believe the context was the issue of inclusion and Jesus's willingness to be present among those whom his society rejected.

This church was a very accepting community, and most of the responses I received after the sermon were positive. But a couple of weeks later a man in the church took me aside and told me that another man had confided in him that he was quite upset by my sermon. He was OK about our adopting biracial children, but he did not think homosexuality should be tolerated. I noted that this person did not speak to me directly and apparently did not criticize my breaking with monogamy.

In the late 1980s I joined a discussion group on gender issues in our local congregation. This months-long educational series focused on learning about sexual orientation, gay and lesbian sub-cultures, and various views on sexual ethics. One of the benefits of this process was that more people in our congregation began to understand why it is important for gays, lesbians and bisexuals to come out. After a period of intentionally informing ourselves about homosexuality, the Unitarian Universalist Community Church was certified as a "Welcoming Congregation" in 1996.

Although I came out to my colleagues at the University and was open about my bisexuality at the Unitarian Universalist Church, I was not generally open in the broader community where we lived. Probably few if any of my neighbors knew. Much of my research on bisexuality was published in major psychological journals, which occasionally prompted calls from TV talk shows inviting me to appear, including "The Phil Donahue Show" and "The Oprah Winfrey Show." After checking with Melissa, I discussed the opportunity with our children. Nathan and Michelle were 9 or 10 years old at the time. Nathan had strong feelings on the subject: "My friends wouldn't care," he said, "but I'm afraid some of their parents might make a fuss. They might not let my friends see me or come to our house."

I took his feelings seriously, and assured him I would not be on either show in a way that would identify me as a bisexual. In one show, I agreed to appear only as a researcher; I did not share my personal story. The other show suggested that I appear with my visual image silhouetted and my voice audio electronically disguised. I agreed to that arrangement. As far as we know, neither show had any repercussions for our children.

It seemed strange to me that people in a racially integrated area would still treat the LBGT community, another oppressed minority, as inferior, and that to protect my children as racial minorities I needed to hide my own status as a sexual minority.

In the period from 1981, when AIDS was first recognized, until the end of the 1990s, when relatively effective anti-viral drug treatments were developed, sixteen of my gay friends and acquaintances died of AIDS-related causes. I know other helping professionals, those who live in the "gay ghettos," who have experienced a hundred or more such deaths. Although the period was a hard one for me, the toll for persons who drew almost all their friendships and support from within the gay community was much heavier. Unlike them, I spent much of my time and got much of my support from within the largely heterosexual community, so my day-to-day existence was not filled with constant reminders of the gay plague.

When AIDS was first recognized in the United States, I was 42 and very active in the gay scene in Chicago. Almost all of the men I knew who had died from AIDS-related causes were younger than I. Any time I visit a person who is dying, or attend a funeral, I am reminded of my own mortality; I am forced to ask myself whether I am living the kind of life I believe in. But deaths that occur unnaturally early are especially likely to trigger self-reflection. Why should this happen? Why did this young person have to die? I also identify with the parents: to witness the death of your own child must be one of the worst tragedies in life. And what of my own survival? Why am I fortunate enough to still be living?

In these deaths there is also the powerful reminder that, unless I am consistent in living out what I know about HIV prevention, I could potentially infect Melissa. Or I could die, leaving Melissa and my family grieving. In a sense, this is a side benefit of being bisexual: I am constantly aware that I must not only take care of my own health, but must also protect Melissa's.

~ ~ ~

Governors State University's undergraduates in psychology were required to take two courses that focused on personal or interpersonal growth, using experiential approaches. Typically these courses were taught in concentrated formats such as weekend labs, which intensified the group process and the students' involvement. A course I taught called "Alternative Lifestyles" met for a series of weekends. At each session, a guest couple or individual I'd invited explained their lifestyle. We covered topics such as celibacy, open marriage, gay male couples, lesbian couples, transsexuals, communal living, and commuter marriages. Late in the course, I told the students about my own bisexual lifestyle. They were curious and asked many questions but rarely expressed antagonism.

Students frequently asked me, "Is your marriage open for you, but not for your wife?"

I responded, "Melissa has the same rights I do to explore other partners, personally and intimately. But Melissa has decided she does not want outside sexual relationships. She wants monogamy for herself, although she accepts that my bisexuality leads me to want an open marriage."

One professor in our department had a primary relationship with a woman, although the two of them were not married. One evening, over a meal with Melissa and me, he told us that sometimes he and his partner participated in swinging. He knew a faculty couple in another university town who often held swinging parties in their large home; we met the couple when all six of us had dinner together. My colleague repeatedly urged Melissa and me to try a swinging party. But this lifestyle did not appeal to us. In Melissa's case, it went against her desire to limit sex to deeply intimate relationships. I was not averse to recreational sexual encounters with men, but I preferred to develop a friendship or at least a sense of personal comfort and sharing first. Swinging seemed to me contrived at best and sexist at worst.

The great anthropologist Margaret Mead commented

that the tradition of lifetime monogamy might have made sense in societies where individuals rarely went through serious changes in their identity. But in today's society, it is rather unlikely that a person can predict what her/his identity will be decades into the future. Mead suggested that most people need different partners at different stages of their lives.

Making a life commitment is only possible if each of the partners can promise to love a changing person. Melissa and I have wanted to stay together because our love has been expansive enough to accept each other, affirming the changes we have made in our identities. Since I feel sure Melissa is capable of continuing to love me even as my identity has changed and may continue to change, I am able to pledge to live with Melissa till death us do part.

I do not take this for granted. I feel truly blessed by the generosity of her love. Love is, at the deepest level, a manifestation of grace: undeserved. Yet, as a bisexual man, I cannot live a full life by "keeping only unto her," as the traditional wedding vows say. The words we chose when we married were "Will you, in spite of all others, remain constant unto her as long as you both shall live?" These words don't clearly state "only," but in fact, we both expected to live monogamously. When I later broke that expectation, I did it with honesty, never deceiving her. But I know that my doing so was painful and frightening for Melissa at the time.

In the open marriage that Melissa and I had worked out, at first I felt that it would be better for both of us if she also had other partners. I thought it was fair, but it was based on a false premise: that the form of intimacy that works for me should also work for her. Melissa's response was sharp: "If you want me to have an outside partner to assuage your guilt, that's not a good reason." Melissa made it clear that she did not want to experiment. "You are a pluralist," she proclaimed, "but I am a monist."

There was no reason we couldn't love each other deeply, despite our differences, and it was shortsighted of me to think she would become like me in her desire for other partners. Monogamy fits her. She wants or needs only one man. I am extremely grateful that I am that one man!

Melissa was certainly correct that I am a pluralist in the sense that I relish experimenting with all kinds of relationships. Our move to an open marriage led to my becoming curious about sex with other women. The obvious context in which to do this was at conferences and workshops. At one therapists' conference, I was in a small group with a woman I had talked with the previous year. We clearly had an emotional rapport, so I invited her to dinner. She accepted. Over dinner, I sensed her sexual interest in me and brought up my bisexuality quite deliberately. She seemed comfortable with that. I casually mentioned my wife and children, to discourage any hope she might have for a lasting relationship. Our conversation flowed easily. I invited her to come back to my room, and we spent the night together. Our interaction was warm and pleasant, spiced by the excitement of a new area of exploration, but it was not really special except in the sense that it was the first time I had pursued a sexual extramarital relationship with a woman.

A year later, at the same conference, we saw each other again, and she proposed that we go out to dinner together, but that we leave it at that. This seemed right for both of us.

Although at first the idea of an open marriage seemed freeing to me, I believe it is much easier to handle polyamory in the gay male subculture than in heterosexual relationships. Although Melissa and I continue to have an open marriage, I use our agreement only for sexual relationships with men. The only woman I continue to have a sexual relationship with is Melissa.

In the summer of 1986, my friend and former student Ted and I again hit the road together to attend a Men and Masculinity conference on a college campus near Atlanta, where we roomed together. On the second day of the conference, Ted came running up to me.

"I've just met a wonderful man," he shouted, "and I know he's just right for YOU."

"Sure," I said. "All I need is to fall in love with someone from some far off state!"

"No, he's not from far away," Ted replied. "He's from Chicago!" Ted excitedly described his new acquaintance. "Ben is only a year older than you, is brilliant like you, and is very warm and outgoing. He's also married, like us. The only possible problem I see is that he's Jewish."

"I'm practically Jewish myself," I laughed. "I was in Hillel Club in college. That's no problem. So how do I meet him?"

"I invited him to join us for lunch."

When Ben and I met, we both agreed that Ted was right. We had so much in common and so much to talk about, and both of us were talkers! His words and mine tumbled all over each other, like two boys rolling down a grassy hill. A few months later, we were tumbling all over each other physically in his bed on the north side of Chicago.

Ben and I were equals intellectually. Theologically and politically we were both liberals. We both loved nature and spirituality. But we did not rush into a sexual relationship. Getting to know each other was exciting in itself, and we did not need sex to sustain our infatuation.

I can still remember the sunny bedroom in Ben's house where we first made love together. I was ecstatic about the relationship. *Finally I am with a man I deeply respect, but also a man who understands my wish to continue my loving marriage with Melissa.* Ben was immersed in his work in a residential treatment center for disturbed kids, and we both enjoyed sharing stories of our clients and our clinical decisions. For months our relationship continued with increasing enthusiasm.

One morning the phone rang. It was Ben, calling to cancel our date that evening. Then he asked that we stop seeing each other altogether. His request came from out of the blue and without explanation. It felt like the strong bond between us, which seemed to me to be as secure as a bungee cord, turned out to be a paper chain that snapped apart due to some slight movement that I hadn't even noticed.

Never in my life had I been this deeply involved and so suddenly dropped. I was heartbroken and mystified. I was in free fall, and there was no bungee cord to pull me back up.

At this point in our marriage Melissa still feared I might leave her (although I never felt I would do that). She did not want to know details of my gay relationships. So I tried on my own to handle Ben's about-face. Melissa has always been sensitive to my moods and needs, so I was sure that she realized something was terribly wrong.

~ ~ ~

Years went by. One day I came home to a message on my answering machine. It was Ben's voice. My heart jumped the moment I heard it:

"I owe you a big apology," he began. "I want to meet with you somewhere neutral to apologize in person, and – if you're willing – to resume our friendship."

When we reconnected by phone to set up a meeting, he said that it wasn't right for him to restart a sexual relationship with me, but he hoped that we could invest in our friendship again. I did not pretend that I wasn't disappointed, but I very much wanted us to be friends, and I was moved that he had finally decided to apologize. Since we had last seen each other, he had undergone a quadruple coronary bypass. During his recovery, while reviewing his life and his hopes for the future, he realized he had wronged me and wanted to reconcile. From this point on, our relationship grew, eventually becoming one of the deepest and most important male/male friendships in my life.

~ ~ ~

Melissa urged me to spend just one evening a week on my involvement in gay life. If she knew when I'd be out, she would be able to plan something she could do, rather than passively waiting for my return. One evening a week seemed pitifully little time to get to know what was becoming such an important part of me. I had spent thirty-nine years living as a heterosexual. Now I felt I had discovered a missing part of myself, and I passionately wanted to devote my time and energy to it. But as Melissa and I negotiated, I became resigned. "Okay, I'll experiment with one evening a week, but I want us to be flexible about which evening. It will depend on when some particular event is happening," I said. In my mind I was saying *and when a particular guy is available.*

Melissa countered, "That will make it nearly impossible for me to plan things to do that interest *me*. I need to schedule events that get me focused on enjoying things, and not thinking about your other life."

Although both of us had strong feelings about this issue, we sincerely tried to understand each other's point of view. We eventually settled on Friday afternoons and evenings as the time for my other life.

For months, maybe even a year, the concrete elements of this agreement helped Melissa. But eventually she realized that setting boundaries on the time I was out did not get at her deeper fears. She expressed the real threat it in writing: "Our old [marriage] contract is void; we are presently operating without a contract or covenant. It is time to create a new one, agree on it, celebrate it, and live it out – without the pain and suffering [we have been experiencing]."

We needed more than a new structure. We needed to redefine our marriage.

CHAPTER 17
MARRYING MY WIFE AGAIN

Could Melissa and I work out a new marriage contract? We both hoped so. We needed some broader clarification of our intentions and commitments, something that expressed, to each other and to those with whom we were closest, what we were experimenting with, as well as the love and generosity that we knew undergirded it. We had confided in two ministers about our marital struggles around my bisexual life. We each trusted them both. One was our long-term friend from our Boston University days, Dr. Garth Mundle, whom we had visited in Toronto after my first sexual encounter with a man. The other minister was local: the Rev. Joe Agne lived in our University community and was pastor of an interdenominational and interracial congregation which I sometimes attended. He had spoken out in support of Christians affirming les-bi-gay relationships.

Together Melissa and I met with Joe to put into writing key elements of a new covenant between us. Our plan was to develop this covenant and then share it in a second marriage ceremony, re-committing ourselves before a group of our most trusted friends.

As we prepared for the ceremony, Melissa spoke more clearly about what she felt truly threatened our marriage. It was not so much that I was bisexual, but that gay liberation had become my social cause. She had long known the depth of my commitment to social justice. My previous involvements, most especially my trip into the south in 1968, gave her the sense that I might abandon her and surrender my life to the cause.

Melissa's concern was a real one. I had a sense that the

civil rights movement was so important that some of us activists might be called to give our lives. In the late 1970s, with my own acceptance of my bisexuality, the issue of social justice had taken on more personal meaning than had my previous work for racial justice. I was now fighting for my own oppressed minority group.

I strongly believed that I should be willing to devote my all, to risk my life for this issue. Now Melissa, my civil-rights activist sister Carol, and my concerned mother cautioned me to move slowly and not take greater risks than necessary, both for Melissa's sake and for the children.

It became clear that we needed some intimate ceremony that placed supportive people around us. The second wedding emerged, first of all, out of the deep love Melissa and I shared. But we also knew I needed help in moving slowly. The ceremony could also provide a way for me to be open in a contained group, so I would be less likely to act precipitously in the larger community.

At this point in our relationship Melissa no longer believed that she could be the primary love in my life. She had decided to settle for less than that, but she wanted to clarify what she could have and make it a sacred commitment through this ceremony. She wrote, "If I can have the assurance and trust that your commitment to me will not be usurped by your activity in gay life, political and personal, it won't be necessary for me to ask that I be the primary value in your life, which I know I can't be. I must have your time and energy and know your commitment in our day-to-day relationships. Your activity regarding gayness must not take away from your life with me; neither must it add anything to our life together."

Melissa's concern about adding anything to our life meant that I must not initiate discussions that involved her in decisions concerning my gay life. She wanted no part in that. Our marital life needed to focus on us, not on my outside relationships.

We invited nine people to a ritual of celebration held in January of 1978. Dave and Jenny Crispin and Bill and Shirley Katz were the couples we had become closest to since we'd moved to Illinois. Joe Agne had given us emotional support through our struggle with my bisexuality; he came with his wife Chris. We had invited both Garth and Dorothy Mundle, who were our first confidants in that struggle and had been important friends since our Boston days, but Dorothy was unable to come. Finally there was a colleague and friend both Melissa and I respected, Dr. Wayne Anderson.

Joe and Garth, both ordained ministers, conducted the ceremony. The meal was catered by Don Day, a wonderful cook from our Unitarian Universalist church. An elementary school teacher, he had been single all his life and was private about his being gay. It was a pleasure to have him present. He made a beautiful wedding cake as part of the celebration.

We also designed new wedding rings, which were made by a silversmith. Each of our rings consists of a broken piece of sterling silver. Its two jagged ends overlap and meld into one circle. This symbolizes our separate identities and the wholeness that comes from our intertwined lives. In addition, Melissa's ring has at the crown two small spheres of silver; mine has three. The first two represent, for each of us, our two primary commitments: to each other, and to our children. Specifically, the first sphere on my ring stands for my commitment to Melissa, and the second for my commitment to Nathan and Michelle. The third sphere on my ring symbolizes my commitment to human liberation, especially to les-bi-gay liberation.

In the ceremony, Melissa urged me to "remember in

love that old commitments are no less precious because they are older." I vowed that "none of my three commitments, to Melissa, to the kids, or to the ministry of liberation, shall supersede the others in any lasting way. Even in temporary situations, none shall supersede the others without careful negotiation and consideration of the others." Despite Melissa's belief that she could no longer be primary, my vows stated, "You are the only one with whom I intend to spend my whole life...there are no major areas of my being which are not known to you. You can hear a new issue in my life, and understand it in the total context of my life."

It was a beautiful ceremony. Every word was appropriate and personal, each line our own composition. And once again we felt the deep support of people who surrounded us with acceptance and love.

~ ~ ~

For both Melissa and me, talking through a series of rules and making agreements helped keep us together. Our second marriage was not magical. A lot of practical and detailed decisions had to be made for years afterward. The new marriage clarified our continuing love and commitment to each other, providing a platform on which to build new agreements.

For example, we found it was important to be clear about what time we would both return from our Friday nights out. If either of us had to be late coming home, we would call and explain or leave a phone message, so the one waiting would not have uncomfortable fantasies about abandonment.

If tension emerged about our separate times or about our communication afterwards, we would set up a specific meeting to reconnect and to talk it through. We'd choose a time when we would not feel pressure about children or work and make sure the appointment was in our datebooks so the issue would not be left hanging.

As we became more comfortable in our new marriage, Melissa began to deepen her friendship with Bill Katz. We both deeply respected Bill, to whom I had confided my bisexuality. His home became a safe place for Melissa on evenings when I was out or at home with gay friends.

Melissa and I also decided to schedule time each week just for us. If two events could be scheduled for the same day, we gave priority to the one we could do together. And at Melissa's request, we agreed that our marriage bed was sacred and off-limits for my activities with a gay partner.

For me, the exploration of new territory or new interests is always exciting, but for Melissa my love of exploration can be frightening. To reduce her fear, I made promises not to jump blindly into some adventure, but to talk it over first with a straight friend whom Melissa respected. Melissa made a careful list of "behaviors that you do that let me know you are still interested in me" and "behaviors that indicate you are 'elsewhere' and I am nonexistent in your life." Her ability to describe the specific behaviors that triggered her fears was extremely helpful, since some of those behaviors had different meanings for me.

I also tend to talk about my feelings and experiences with people, sometimes in Melissa's presence, without thinking through how Melissa might react. So I agreed to prepare Melissa in advance if I were going to discuss my other life – for example, if one of my siblings or friends were to visit us. Even with preparation, this could become threatening for Melissa, and I agreed not to criticize her if she decided to leave the room when the subject came up or when the subject went on too long for her to bear.

We installed a second phone line for my private practice, and I gave out that number, rather than the home phone number, to my gay friends. This reduced the likelihood of Melissa's answering the phone and accidently having to converse with one of them. Meanwhile Melissa agreed to work toward accepting my bisexuality, not just tolerating it.

When making important life decisions that affect each other or the children, we committed ourselves to discussing them carefully with each other, each listening intently to the personal meaning of the decision for the other. We involve trusted people in discussions at each major decision point before taking any action.

I don't want to give the impression that our approach to practical decision-making would work for all couples. I believe it works for us because of the levels of deep trust and honest communication that have developed over the years. But I do believe trust and honesty alone are not enough, and Melissa's urgency to be sure decisions are clearly communicated and negotiated has helped our uncommon marriage succeed.

Five years later, I was able to write to other couples struggling with open bisexual marriages, "We now feel confident our own marriage is a stable one.... It *is* possible to maintain a mixed-orientation marriage in which each partner can function with integrity." This confidence came partly out of recognizing that the fantasy I once had of having two equal partners, one male and one female, would not work for Melissa and me. Melissa needed to be primary if our marriage was to last. The idea of two equal partnerships simultaneously may work for a while in some rare couples, as in the an earlier portrait of a bisexual marriage, *Barry and Alice* (Kohn, 1980). But even their remarkable marriage later broke apart when Alice found a straight man seeking monogamy. In our second marriage I vowed to make Melissa my primary partner.

Our children were only eight at the time of our second marriage. I began spending a period each week alone with each of them. I had been preoccupied with the gay issue; now it was time to rebuild the bonds within the family. Melissa's ability to structure and organize helped me become a better parent, especially in my conflicted relationship with Nathan.

In 1984 Melissa resigned from her position as head nurse at a local hospital, and I took a year's sabbatical. Both of us worked only part time so that we could complete a program in marriage and family counseling with Wayne Anderson. Our goal was to develop the skills to work together as co-therapists. Training and studying together helped us strengthen the bonds of our marriage. We were both certified as marriage and family counselors in 1985. In 1985, Melissa and I and our two 15-year-olds moved to a larger house in the woods, and I gave up my office in the bank building and began seeing my counseling clients at home. But that meant I no longer had a separate place to entertain my gay friends or partners. Of course I never invited gay friends home unless I knew that Melissa, Nathan and Michelle would be away.

CHAPTER 18
A SPECIAL FRIEND AND A STRANGE FAUN

In the late 1980s Michael, an old friend from my seminary days, came to Chicago to catalogue and interpret the findings of an archeological excavation he had participated in earlier.

Soon after his arrival, I phoned him and invited him to go with me to hear a speaker we both admired. After the event we stopped for dessert, and as we talked I was reminded of how much we had in common: a love of music and drama, similar theological and political views, and a deep sense of integrity in relationships. Although his resonant bass voice rarely revealed his humorous side, several times during our conversation he flashed a wry smile. The collar button of his dress shirt was open, and a tuft of hair suggested Michael had a very hairy chest, a turn-on for me. I drove him back to his apartment and he invited me in. What a wonderful reunion, to move so seamlessly from years of not seeing each other to warm and exuberant sex. As delightful as this was, at the time I had no idea that this could become a lasting relationship. It worked because he already knew Melissa, he respected our marriage, and we both accepted that it was likely to end when he left Chicago to return to his regular teaching position. I think we both expected that any long-lasting gay relationship would require both men to reside in the same city. And I think we both fantasized that a lasting gay partner would be similar in personality to ourselves. Although we had common interests, Michael viewed himself as an archetypal introvert and perceived me as an extreme extravert. But as the years passed Michael became more comfortable in social situations – he credits me for showing him how. And I became more conscious of limiting the time I am center stage.

Michael and I had a number of meals together over the two semesters he was in Chicago. We attended a concert or two and went for walks in a city park. Usually our meetings led to sex. Although I don't like the gay culture's obsession with looks, when we were in bed I appreciated that he kept his body trim and his muscles hard. Our relationship became increasingly intimate and sexual.

That year came very close to fulfilling my image of the ideal love life for a bisexual. My fantasy had been of being in bed with my wife on one side and my gay lover on the other side. I'd spent the year having a deep and fulfilling friendship with a gay partner as well as my emotionally rich relationship with my wife, with a very satisfying sexual relationship with each of them. Both were within reach, living where I could see them regularly.

But even though I wished that the year would go on forever, I knew that the arrangement was *not* ideal for either Michael or Melissa. Michael wished he didn't have to share me with Melissa, although he was never in any way disrespectful of our marriage. Melissa now accepted that she couldn't have me all to herself, but she would have liked my gay life to be far away from home.

In late spring of 1988 Michael had to return to his teaching job in New England, but on his way toward the Indiana border we met for a leisurely afternoon in a motel room on Interstate 80 and a goodbye meal at a nearby restaurant. We both sensed that the relationship would continue, but with miles and months separating our visits. To me this seemed like a honeymoon in reverse; instead of moving in together after the honeymoon, we'd been together more than ever before and then moved hundreds of miles apart.

The following fall Michael made an unexpected trip to

Chicago to present at a conference. He was put up in a large corner room at the Conrad Hilton, with a view of Grant Park. It looked like a bridal suite – and we spent a wonderful afternoon making love. It felt so beautiful to be reconnected with Michael. We'd only been apart five or six months, but it had seemed way too long.

* * *

The gay world was still fairly new and exciting to me, and in some ways, I slid back into my gay adolescence. During a long period between visits with Michael, I began a relationship with another man who also liked singing and acting. Stan and I met by chance in the Art Institute of Chicago, standing side-by-side absorbing the primitive beauty of Gauguin's *Tahitian Landscape #2*. Stan had a small pointed beard similar to Gauguin's in one of his self-portraits.

Somehow I mustered the guts to start a conversation, and I began to suspect that he was gay or bisexual. We spent another hour or more viewing art, then walked together along Chicago's beautiful shoreline. Stan was about ten years younger than I, was also married, and confided that he was confused about how open to be with his wife. We corresponded for a week or two. Then he urged me to come to the north suburbs, where he was performing in a musical.

"My wife will be away one of the nights I'm performing," he wrote. The night before this event, I woke up with a poem in my head. To my amazement, the poem was fully formed, eight verses long, in iambic pentameter and with an AA/BB rhyming pattern! Although the poem needed some minor tweaking, I was able to transcribe all the verses as fast as I could write, with no sense that I was trying to compose them. It felt like some muse was dictating the poem to me.

I Took Both Roads

Oh Wide-eyed Love!

Oh siren, wide-eyed goatee-bearded faun!
Who called you forth from fantasies to haunt
My morning, noon and afternoon and eve,
To keep me giddy – gay without reprieve?

Your wide-eyed look seduces but deceives,
For I am left without perspective. Leave
Me. Give me back a touch of sense
Lest all my acts be aimed at recompense

For youth spent in a haze 'bout what I long for,
then age spent in a maze to redo gone-for
aspirations, fantasies, and longings,
abandoning most precious dear belongings.

Can life be lived by making up the past?
Can love be found by chasing what won't last?
Does reason ask such questions just to taunt?
Does romance now demand "Pursue the hunt"?

"Think not about tomorrow," says the sage.
(I note he did not reach a mature age.)
"Live not in past remorses," says my mind.
I seek the Present. A faun is what I find.

If any sense be made of sense and passion,
Must be that ecstasy cannot be fathomed.
Yet passion is not all there is to love.
The Spirit may be richer than the dove

Who flies into my pathway, bids me follow,
But makes no promises about tomorrow.
And so I'll walk my pathway day by day,

Admitting I don't know a better way.

I'll follow *both* the passion and the love,
Both riches of the Spirit and the dove,
Until they each, or both, split from my center,
And pain and loneliness then bid me enter.

I interpreted this poetic creativity to be a portent of the budding of an important relationship. Although I was already involved in a long-term relationship with Michael, I was excited by the possibility of a local relationship to complement our long-distance one.

As long as I am honest with both of them, I can manage two relationships, I told myself.

I headed northward, having typed out the poem to show Stan. We didn't get a chance to meet before the performance. He was delightful in his role on stage, which only added to my growing infatuation.

But when I met him afterward, he was already backpedaling. "I think it's better we don't go to my home," he said. "I've made a reservation for you at a nearby motel."

After he escorted me into the motel, he said that his work schedule was too busy, so we wouldn't be able to spend time together the next morning. He was the muse for my poem, but didn't seem to want to continue the relationship.

The experience of a poem arising fully-formed was so remarkable that during my next visit with Michael I blurted out the whole event. Although I didn't realize it at the time, the story of my infatuation and the muse-inspired poem hurt Michael deeply

When Michael finally told me years later, I understood that the poem was the gift of infatuation, not love. My love for Michael was and is far richer and more mature than this short-lived fantasy love with Stan. The last six lines of the poem speak of a decision to move one step at a time, but the implied fear is that I'll lose not only the object of my infatuation, but also Melissa and Michael, and end up painfully lonely. Instead, I lost Stan, but both Melissa and Michael, although they experienced hurt and suffering, stayed with me.

For a number of years, I developed various relationships while seeking a Chicago-area person as a gay lover. I still saw Michael. Throughout this time, my mother was still living in Western New York, and once or twice a year I drove to her home for a few days and then drove on to Michael's place in New England. My visits were brief, but we grew increasingly close. I was so grateful that we could stay connected.

We frequently attended musical events or theater together. He had some experience as a performer, both in acting and in choral music. I loved both music and drama, but I was an observer rather than a performer. Michael and I had similar perspectives on religion and politics, and certainly on civil rights issues. On the latter I was more the activist and he the observer.

My relationship with Michael remained a very positive one. I was especially grateful that it combined friendship and gay sex in a way that I'd previously experienced only with Ben. Further, this relationship had a chance of lasting, since I regularly visited the area where my mother and some of my cousins lived. My routine of visiting Michael when I drove east to see Mom once or twice a year continued until 2000, when we siblings decided we needed to move Mom to a place where she could have more care.

But at this point neither my libido nor my heart was ready to settle for a long-distance lover who I'd see only three or four times a year. I did not think of Michael as a steady or exclusive relationship. I still had some important growing up to do on the gay side before settling down.

CHAPTER 19
HOMOPHOBIA AND MEN SUPPORTING MEN

My life with Melissa changed dramatically in 1988. Both Michelle and Nathan left home to begin college, moving to dormitories on campus (and repeating the pattern my mother had encouraged for myself and my sibs).

In addition, Melissa and another nurse began a new business, a pediatric home health care agency. Within a few years they had satellite offices in nine different cities in four states. Because Melissa was intensely involved in assuring the high quality of nursing care, she consistently worked 60 to 70 hours a week for almost a decade. She eventually hired Lois, a very competent nurse who in time became the CEO/President of the company. But Melissa's workload continued to be very demanding.

About five years into my professorship at GSU I was asked to meet with the University president, Leo Goodman-Malamuth. Our relationship had always been a friendly one. When I entered his office he greeted me warmly, and after a little social banter he mentioned that the University was in the midst of a fund drive and that he had received a phone call from a regular contributor. The caller requested that the president fire me! The contributor had seen me in the media, had learned that I was open on campus about being bisexual, and had tried to persuade the president that such a person should not be allowed to teach.

"I explained to her that I had no grounds to fire you," the president said. "I told her that your teaching evaluations were excellent, that you had a very strong research record, and that you were fully qualified to teach in both psychology and counseling." Looking me in the eye, he continued, "I thought you should know that this happened, but as you know I fully support your continuing here." He ended the conversation by giving me a big hug. I left feeling grateful and relieved.

Of course I occasionally had to deal with criticism from students, as well. In one of my counseling courses we discussed client issues that often pose problems for counselors new to the field. The issue of homosexual clients came up, and I mentioned that I was myself bisexual and had focused my recent research on the subject.

Our counseling classes tended to be small and informal; many students in the more advanced courses had known me from prerequisite courses. This new information about my life led to a number of students asking questions, both professional and personal. One student commented, "But you have mentioned raising adopted kids. I thought you were married."

This seemed to be a teaching moment. I explained that I had been open with my wife about my bisexuality even before we adopted the kids. So far as I can remember, all the students' questions centered on the honesty of my relationship with Melissa. No one asked intimate questions about sexual acts, either homosexual or heterosexual.

At the last session of the class, a month later, I passed out the required Student Evaluation of Instructor (SEI) forms. When the typed summaries of the SEIs were returned to me several weeks later with the students' identification removed, I was shocked that my average scores were considerably below my usual ratings. When I looked at the transcribed comments, three of the students had made negative remarks about my "sharing inappropriate personal material" in the classroom. Almost identical wording occurred in each of the three. In every category of evaluation of my teaching, their numeric ratings were at the lowest level. It appeared that three students had conspired together to punish me for disclosing my bisexuality.

I made sure that Dr. Woodward, the chair of the department, saw the individual SEIs so he could understand my low average scores. Since my evaluations had generally been high, and since the process of faculty advancement and payment had been carefully structured in negotiations between the union and the administration, I had no real worry that these evaluations could threaten my job security or reputation. However, the incident confirmed the wisdom of my delaying coming out until I had tenure, as friends on the faculty and administration had advised.

For years I was the only openly LBGT faculty member, so it was not uncommon for students I would not normally come into contact with to seek me out to confide that they were LBGT and to ask for my feedback concerning which faculty were homophobic and in which courses it was safe to disclose being LBGT. I also received referrals in my private practice from Chicago gay organizations, because I was one of the few therapists in the south suburbs knowledgeable about working with les-bi-gay clients.

~ ~ ~

I was grateful for the affirmation from my workplace and my UU congregation, but I also felt a need for a men's support group. So two of my male friends and I decided to start one.

The group began with eleven men. Six of them were straight, and five were either gay or bi. We ranged in age from late twenties to sixties. One of us was African-American, one of South Asian descent, and the rest were Caucasian. Our religious backgrounds included Roman

Catholic (one man had studied for the priesthood), Protestant, Unitarian Universalist, Hindu, and atheist. Our occupations included mortician, medical doctor, academic administrator, student affairs director, college professor, librarian, counselor, psychologist, and tree farmer. What we had in common was an awareness that male gender roles had affected us and an openness to grow personally and interpersonally. For many of the straight men in the group, it was the first chance they had had to get to know gay or bisexual men. For many of the gay or bi men, it was a rare chance to become trusting and open in the presence of straight men.

After the group had met for several months, the gender-related issues became less important. One of the men in the group, Bill Dodd, developed terminal cancer. He shared deeply his attitude about his own death, and his gratitude for the deeply satisfying life he had led. The group also led to my close friendship with George Ochsenfeld, another activist. We connected because of a shared commitment to human liberation for all races and religions, for both sexes, and for both gays and straights. Our friendship has been one of the longest male friendships in my life.

Shortly after Bill Dodd's death George and I attended the memorial service at GSU, where Bill had been an administrator. As people rose to speak about Bill, one man said something that was (unintentionally) heterosexist. At that point, I felt compelled to speak. Without directly referring to what had just been said, I stated that I had deeply appreciated Bill's friendship, his comfort level concerning his own sexuality, and his willingness to be understanding and accepting of gays and bisexuals, including me. Although I was open about being bisexual at the University, I had never stated it in the presence of many non-university people from the community, so I felt exposed in this setting. When I returned to my seat beside George, I put my arm around his shoulders in friendship – not thinking of how that might look to those around me. George is a straight man, but those who did not know him and saw me put my arm around him might have thought he was my gay lover. George later told me that he was aware of that, but he risked it because he knew I was feeling vulnerable. It proved to me that he was a true ally, someone who will stand with the oppressed at the risk of being treated as one of them and suffering oppression himself.

It is rare that American men dare to be affectionate and intimate with other men or risk being vulnerable and asking for nurturance from other men. One of the male students in my undergraduate Adolescent Psychology class, seeing slides of Indian street scenes showing pairs of men walking hand in hand, asked, "Is being gay more common there?"

"No," I replied, "but sustaining deep male-to-male friendships is more common." How much of American men's fear of being close to other men comes from identifying it with being gay? The process men undergo when they let in the feminine, letting go of barriers and expectations, is not just a psychological release. It involves opening up to a broader view of manhood than the limited roles portrayed by super-masculine icons. New receptivity in a man permits him to sense other's needs and to be nurturing. Gradually the man becomes less armored and easier to touch, so he himself receives more nurturing. Perhaps this is why the Spirit, in much of Christian tradition, is viewed as feminine.

CHAPTER 20
INDIA

Melissa knew that I had long wanted to visit India, and even though she had no interest in going herself, she wanted to see me fulfill one of my life desires.

In 1990, I prepared to take my sabbatical leave in India. My close friend Ben had applied to teach English for three years at a university in Jakarta. He wanted to see India as well, so I suggested we meet there while he was living in Indonesia. Another friend, John Speaks, spent six months every year in India and had offered to give me a guided tour. He said he would plan a tour for the three of us through the Himalayas and other areas in the north.

I also was close to a faculty colleague from India, Dr. Jagdish P. Davé. J.P., as we called him, had previously lived in Ahmedabad, Gandhi's home city. J.P. embodied the melding of psychology and spirituality and of East and West and was an inspiration for many of our students. He helped me plan the first part of my trip, connecting me with his friend Mr. Patel in Ahmedabad. I would fly into Delhi, go on to Ahmedabad for several weeks to live with the Patel family, and then meet Ben and John to travel together through the Himalayas.

A year before the trip, I learned that there was a small newspaper published for gay and bisexual men in Southeast Asia. I subscribed and found occasional classified ads by men in India wanting to correspond with American men. Several lived in cities I planned to visit on my trip. I wrote to three or four of them. At this time India was just beginning to develop a more open gay subculture. Two decades had passed since the Stonewall Bar rebellion that launched the gay movement in US, and gays and bisexuals in India were envious and deferential toward American gays.

When I arrived at the airport in Delhi, I was met by Sunil, with whom I'd been corresponding for several months. Besides being bisexual, Sunil was trained as a travel agent and offered to help me work out details of my trip in the Himalayas. He was knowledgeable about gay liberation in America and longed for a sexual relationship with an American. I was attracted to Sunil's beautiful eyes and dark brown skin, but I was exhausted from the long flights and needed to overcome my jet lag. When Sunil and I reconnected for breakfast the following morning, I found him a very enjoyable, warm person. A gradual move into a sexual relationship ensued. Much of my awake time for the next four days was spent touring old and new Delhi with my guide, this friendly, attractive younger man.

Young Indian men like Sunil, new to the gay world, often choose an older partner, similar to the mentor relationships of classical Greece. An older Western gay or bi man is especially desirable. At the time of my trip, functioning as bisexual rather than gay was the norm in Asian gay culture. Even when the family knows or senses that a son is gay, they expect him to marry a woman. Sunil was quite comfortable with his own homosexuality, as long as it didn't interfere with his family life.

My next stop, a brief trip to Mumbai, was focused on seeing Elephanta Island, with its ancient caves of huge early Hindu sculptures. On the boat I met Eleanor, a British woman some years older than me. As we walked into the cave together, I was awed by the huge ancient stone sculpture against the far wall. It depicted God as having three faces. I knew it had nothing to do with the Christian trinity. It seemed to me to convey that Shiva could look in all directions – could see all sides to an issue. The sculpture was absolutely beautiful, yet it was not heroic, like the Greek and Roman sculptures of men. Shiva seemed almost androgynous, both feminine and masculine.

I think Eleanor realized how much I was moved. On the return boat ride, we sat across a table from each other and chatted as we ate lunch. I was conscious that her eyes were sending sexual messages: not seductive or coy, but definitely sensual. My mind flashed back to a situation decades earlier when, as a college freshman on the beach in Ocean City, an older woman, burdened with marriage to a now partially paralyzed husband, had sent me similar messages. At that time, I was inexperienced and not ready to respond positively. This time I could have. For reasons not clear to me, I chose not to.

When I arrived at Mr. and Mrs. Patel's home in Ahmedabad, it was immediately clear that his business of developing private elementary schools was very successful. The beautiful white granite mansion in a large gated yard was impressive. I was given a lovely bedroom and the full attention of a young male servant to bring me water, hang up my clothes, and make sure I was comfortable.

So began my time in the city in which Gandhi had grown up. The state teachers college in Ahmedabad provided a site for the research topic for my sabbatical: conducting a psychological study of young Indian women's preferences for arranged or Western-style marriages. And living with the Patels and getting to know their adult children and their grandchildren gave me deeper insight into the nature of the three-generational extended Indian family.

Mr. Patel was the patriarch of a family consisting of his wife, a married daughter and her husband and child, and an unmarried adult son still living in the home. They were all wonderful hosts, and Mr. Patel, although only a decade older than I, treated me like one of his sons.

I connected by phone with a gay Indian man with whom I had corresponded, a student in a technical college. He offered to take me to the local gay meeting place, a straight bar which hosted gays one evening a week. My hosts had no idea about my interest in India's emerging gay community. So they were surprised when an incredibly handsome college student, Sohan, came on his motorcycle to pick me up late one afternoon. I said something vague about my doing research on different college and technical campuses.

My relationship with Sohan was completely platonic – which is not to say that I didn't have fantasies, riding behind him on his motorcycle with my arms circling his waist while he sped through the congested streets of the city. Although the monsoon season was officially over, on one of our trips together we were drenched by a sudden downpour. I had been trying to adjust to the sizzling heat of India and found the rain refreshing; Sohan was freezing and urged me to hold him close to keep him warm. That was easy.

One of Sohan's close friends, Brandon, had been an actor in Australia. He had fallen in love with India while traveling around the country with a Shakespearean troupe. Now he directed a large agency that provided services, food, and other supplies for economically needy people. He also owned a peacock farm in a wooded area outside the city.

Brandon threw a gay party at his large farmhouse, and Sohan made sure I was invited. At this party I had a moving experience of the breaking down of social barriers. Many years back Brandon had come to know a young man of the lowest caste, the Dalits or "untouchables." Aseem was a goat herder who migrated seasonally into the Ahmedabad area. Brandon eventually realized that this slim petite fellow was also gay. Brandon became a mentor for him. On occasions when Aseem returned to the area, he was welcomed as a guest in Brandon's home.

On the day of the party, Sohan mentioned to me that Aseem would be attending. As Sohan and I approached the farm, the noise of Sohan's motorcycle set off the peacocks, which screamed out their raucous cries. When I moved into the living room to join Sohan and some others who were conversing in English, I sat down on an empty couch. Aseem followed me into the room and sat at the other end of the couch. As I turned to acknowledge his presence, I immediately noticed his smile, which seemed natural and welcoming. His shiny white teeth contrasted with his dark brown complexion. A while later, several of the men got up and went to the kitchen to replenish their drinks. Aseem then moved over and sat very close to me.

"Do you speak any English?" I asked him, and he understood enough to shake his head and respond, "Almost no." I appreciated that he didn't seem apologetic. Aseem walked back into the kitchen, and in his absence Brandon commented, "Aseem seems to be attracted to you, Dave. We're very casual here. If he invites you up to the bedroom he is using, feel free to go."

Many of the men had come in couples, and Sohan had gravitated to a group of men about his own age speaking in Gujarati. They moved into the kitchen. When Aseem returned from the kitchen, he sat down to my left. He and I were alone in the room.

We sat for a while in silence. I was struck by the fact that he seemed very relaxed, totally comfortable with the silence. I was attracted to his simple, rural appearance and his very dark complexion. He peered at me occasionally, and I smiled back, enjoying his attention but wishing we had a common language. After a while he gently laid his right hand on my leg, looked me in the eyes, and motioned for me to follow him. As he led me up the stairs he pointed out some framed paintings on the wall, which appeared to be early Indian folk art. I examined them with interest and stood a while looking at the one that I liked most.

Near the top of the stairs, across from a bathroom, Aseem entered a small bedroom with a double bed. He arranged three or four pillows to lean against the headboard and sat down on the bed, leaning against them and leaving room for me to sit beside him. I joined him on the bed. Very gently, he touched my chest and then began to undo a few of my shirt buttons. I began to feel aroused, but I also was surprised how relaxed and comfortable I felt, given this unexpected interaction. I responded by beginning to loosen his shirt. There were no words, yet a constant flow of communication: he was sensitively in touch with me, without any pressure, and I mirrored his sensitivity. Slowly we explored each other. We kept it safe, with no attempt at penetration, but we each reached a gentle orgasm. We lay there relaxed in each other's arms for quite a while.

Silently, I wondered what we might do next. I trusted that Aseem would take the lead. He walked quietly to the bathroom and brought me a towel, went back and washed himself, and returned to the bedroom casually dressed. I followed his lead, washed up, and dressed. As I returned to the bedroom, he stood, approached me slowly, gave me a soft hug, and motioned for me to wait.

He tiptoed down a few stairs in his stocking feet, carefully took something off the wall, and brought it to me. He was holding a primitive handmade bow and a small quiver of arrows, much smaller than the ones used in modern archery. He signaled for me to follow, and escorted me down a back staircase that led directly to the woods. We walked a short way together, away from the house; he led me to a target propped up against a large tree. Standing beside me, he shot the first arrow, which struck near the center of the bull's-eye. Then he handed me the bow and an arrow. It did not feel like a competition, so it didn't bother me that he clearly had practiced this and that his aim was considerably better than my own. What mattered was that we were out in nature together, with something to do that made it comfortable to continue our interaction in silence. I felt so appreciated and so appreciative, being with him in this peaceful way. It seemed as though our colors, cultures, languages, and status no longer mattered. We were simply two men, longing for each other, touching each other, and touched by the simplicity, the authenticity, and the tenderness.

~ ~ ~

From Ahmedabad I traveled to Delhi, where Sunil and I reconnected.

A few days later Sunil went with me to the airport to greet my American friends John and Ben as they arrived from Atlanta and Indonesia respectively. There Sunil and I parted for about a month, knowing we would reconnect in Mumbai during my final week in India.

John, Ben, and I had hired a driver to take us on a tour of some important Indian sites, including two sources of the holy Ganges River up in the Himalayas. All three of us Americans had been involved in the "Men and Masculinity" conferences, were married, and were bisexual. Each of us had been honest with our wives about our bisexuality. Ben was now living in Indonesia, where he'd found the man of his dreams, a Malaysian.

John and his wife were open with each other about his bisexuality, but their arrangements differed from Melissa's and mine. John restricted his homosexual expression to one particular gay friend in America; they spent a month of each year traveling together. So during the period that Ben, John, and I traveled together, we felt a close companionship but did not relate to each other sexually.

The journey in the Himalayas was one of the most remarkable trips of my life. John had done his homework well and took us to places he himself had not seen before, including a view of what climbers consider the most beautiful mountain in the world, Nanda Devi. We spent a couple of nights at a very high altitude in a barely heated cabin. In the bitter cold, we all snuggled together in one double bed to stay warm. I found hot Indian tea with milk and sugar a wonderful way to awaken all my senses on a cold mountain morning.

At my request our itinerary included the erotic temples of Khajuraho. These ancient buildings had lain hidden in the jungles for centuries. I was both aesthetically fascinated and spiritually excited by the erotic sculptures that undulate around their outside walls. Some of the configurations show lesbian sexual interactions, but not gay male sex.

Equally unforgettable is the incredible beauty of some Mughal Islamic architecture. Almost three decades earlier, I had been awed by the Alhambra near Seville. Seeing the Taj Mahal in Agra was even more moving. It is truly one of the most beautiful buildings in the world.

My trip to India was the longest period that I'd spent away from Melissa since we married. I missed her a great deal, especially when I was living in Ahmedabad with the Patel family. Yet my voyage provided a wonderful period of exploring and fulfilled some of my dreams. In many ways it was a pilgrimage for me.

CHAPTER 21
MADLY IN LOVE

Shortly after I returned to the US, I began conducting interviews for another bisexual marriage study. I met the husbands on the northern edge of Chicago in a satellite office of Horizons, the umbrella les-bi-gay organization in Chicago at that time. On one of my first evenings in that office, I was struck by the looks and glowing personality of the man answering the gay information phone lines at the reception desk. When I first glanced at him, I took him to be partially East Indian, although when I looked again I realized he was predominantly African American. I asked him what his racial heritage was. He smiled a delightful impish smile and said, "Of course I am African American, but my grandmother was half Indian." He meant East Indian. My time with Sunil had increased my appreciation of the beauty of dark-skinned men, so meeting a handsome black man on my return (and then learning Antwon's grandmother was half Indian) increased my linking of the exotic and the erotic.

In any case Antwon was charming. He was 39, although he looked younger. I was 52.

After a few more conversations, we began dating. Antwon was only about 5'4" tall, but in addition to being warm and outgoing, he was handsome and a perfect mesomorph – which is to say, "hunky". I had never before dated a man who I felt was so incredibly attractive physically. Antwon was also really fun to be around, interested in many subjects including music and politics, and talented in drawing and painting. He had the Asian youths' predisposition to date men older than themselves.

Unlike many younger men, including those I'd met in

India, Antwon longed for more than a friend with benefits. He was a member of the Jehovah's Witnesses church, which is very homophobic, and he came from a sexually conservative African-American home; he longed for emotional affirmation of his homosexuality and wanted a committed relationship. He hoped eventually to make a living in art, which his family considered impractical. I had been an art connoisseur and amateur collector for years.

Antwon was a volunteer at Horizons. He was unemployed and had a very spotty work history. During the period we dated, he enrolled part time in some college courses to complete a bachelor's degree in art. Despite his self-definition as gay, he was uneasy about sexual relationships; our friendship deepened long before we had any directly sexual interaction. He was the youngest of twelve siblings, and at times I was confused about whether he saw me as a partner, a big brother, or a generous father. When he was without income and living in a group home, I made the deposit and paid his first month's rent for an apartment so he could pursue his art, and so we could have some privacy.

My relationship with Antwon was beautiful in a number of ways. My age and the fact that I was neither athletic nor handsome did not seem to make him less attracted to me. His race and lack of formal education were not barriers for me. We shared not only excitement and fun in outdoor activities, but emotional intimacy and self-disclosure. Both of us loved dancing – Antwon had once stepped in, as a substitute, to dance in a Chicago performance of the Alvin Ailey Dance Theatre – and we enjoyed some fun evenings on the dance floors of gay clubs.

After a couple of months of dating, I picked up on his wish that we make some kind of commitment. As was always the case with men I got involved with, Antwon knew from the start that I was the father of two young adults and was fully committed to continuing my marriage with Melissa. I felt I really loved Antwon, although he knew I would not move in with him but would continue to consider Melissa my primary commitment.

Antwon and I wanted some way to celebrate our deep investment in each other and decided to have our own private ceremony. We picked out matching rings, simple silver ones with a smooth semi-precious gemstone. We chose a sunny summer day to go together to one of our favorite spots, a pier on the Lake Michigan shore, where we privately expressed our love and exchanged rings. For months, I wore the ring Antwon had given me on my right hand and on my left continued to wear the wedding ring Melissa had given me in our re-commitment ceremony.

Almost all of the time Antwon and I spent together was at his new apartment, walking alone in the Lake Michigan beach and park areas, or in gay restaurants or dancing places. Only once, so far as I remember, did Antwon come down to my house. I met him at the train station, and we spent much of the day at our home. Melissa was out of town, so this was in keeping with our agreements.

I looked forward to traveling with him, so we could have some nights together. For years my fantasy as a bisexual man had been to have committed relationships with both my wife and a man. Now it seemed as though my dream had finally been realized.

But soon things were going wrong on both ends of my love life. Melissa was feeling less and less valued, and Antwon was becoming less and less available. There were entire weekends when I couldn't reach him, and when we were together he seemed to want me as a big brother and avoided sexual intimacy.

That year I had been asked along with two others to

keynote an annual Men and Masculinity conference to be held at McCormick Center in Chicago. Each of us was to describe our very different lifestyles: a straight married man, my gay friend Derrik, and me as a bisexual. Antwon came with me to the conference, and we were spending the three days in the McCormick hotel, planning a rare two nights together. The presentation took place fairly early in the program, and in describing my bisexual lifestyle, I had Antwon stand as I introduced him to the whole conference as my lover.

I got the sense that Antwon loved the attention of the audience more than he cared about our being together alone that night. I had thought his anxiety about gay sex had to do with our limited times together; I assumed that a relaxed two nights together would decrease the anxiety. Instead it seemed to amplify it. So once again our sexual experience together was disappointing.

I began to observe a pattern of Antwon disappearing for days at a time. The first time this occurred I called every one of his friends that I knew; none of them had seen him. He and I had planned to meet that week, but when I drove to his apartment to pick him up for dinner, he wasn't there. Since I had a key to his apartment, I let myself in and lay on his bed to take a nap. When I woke up again at least 45 minutes had passed, but he still was not there. As is my habit, I had a novel in the car, so I got it and stayed to read for an additional half hour. Still Antwon did not show.

It was getting dark, and I decided not to waste more time. I left a note reminding him of my phone number and some change to use in a payphone, since he had no phone in the apartment.

Several days later Antwon called me, apologizing but saying everything was OK now and asking me to come to see him in a few days. When I saw him next, what minimal explanation he made did not make sense to me, but I enjoyed being with him again.

Another time he was missing even longer. I worried that he had been mugged. Twice previously, according to his report, he had been in a gay bar, walked out to head home, and was mugged in an alley near the bar. Anti-gay crimes had been frequent in the preceding years, so the story seemed believable, especially because Antwon was a bit of a tease, very attractive, and smaller than most men. We know that much anti-gay violence is perpetuated by men who are aroused by other men but hate this in themselves and transform their hatred into aggression against other gay men.

When almost a week went by with no word, I decided it was wise to file a missing persons report. The Cook County police were not at all sympathetic, accusing me of over-reacting. "After all, he is an adult and has a right to take off without reporting to his friends," the officer argued. I was not about to tell this officer that I considered myself much more than a friend. After several more days, I finally got a call from Antwon asking me to come over. Again I received only minimal explanations, which seemed vague and puzzling.

For Easter, I had a trip planned to visit my mother, who was still living in the house in which I grew up. The week before I left on the ten-hour drive to Mom's, Antwon lost his job (a fairly regular occurrence). Since he was unemployed, we discussed his going with me.

About fourteen years had passed since I had come out to Mom as bisexual, but she had never met any of my partners. I telephoned Mom to check what arrangements she would be comfortable with if Antwon came with me. Usually when I visited Mom's home I slept in the smallest bedroom, which had a single bed. Mom slept in the master bedroom. There was a double bed in the third bedroom. I suggested that Antwon and I could stay in a motel, or we could each sleep in one of the two bedrooms she didn't use.

"It's a silly waste of money to stay in a motel," Mom said. She told me that it was okay with her if Antwon and I slept in the bedroom with the double bed.

I was a bit surprised. "Are you sure?" I asked.

She responded, "Yes, it's up to you two."

I remember bragging to some of my close friends about my mother's amazing tolerance, especially considering that she was 83 and knew almost nothing about the gay world. Decades later I learned that Mom had discussed with close relatives that she was uneasy about my bringing Antwon with me to stay overnight in her home. So even my asking, "Are you sure?" failed to cut through Mom's tendency to please others and slight her own feelings.

A few days before he and I were to leave on the trip, Antwon once again disappeared. By this time I was fed up with his pattern of going missing, reappearing, not explaining, but wanting to reconnect. There was no way I wanted to drag my mother into this drama. So it was clear I needed to make the trip on my own.

Perhaps if I hadn't been so emotionally involved, I would have realized that Antwon was a binge drinker. I finally understood a few weeks after my return from the trip to Mom's. I had lent Antwon an expensive single-lens reflex camera, a gift my youngest brother had purchased for me while in Vietnam. Antwon's first story was that he had taken the camera with him to a gay bar and left it with someone while he was out on the dance floor. As I pushed him about the story, it became clear that he was unconscious for a period; most likely he had passed out at the bar.

I began to put the pattern together. Low self-esteem

or depression led him to self-medicate with alcohol. This often led to his passing out. When he came to, he felt guilty. Sometimes his repentance involved reconnecting with his sister and a renewed involvement with the homophobic church of his childhood and family. Other times he attempted to return to a gay lifestyle with the help of his relationship with me.

After a series of attempts to convince Antwon to commit to treatment for his alcohol problems, I gave up on changing him and began to consider ending the relationship. The last straw was his call to our house at 3:00 a.m. one weekend. Melissa didn't resent it when one of her highly trained nurses called her in the middle of the night because a patient's medical status suddenly changed and the nurse needed help with medical decisions. But when a phone call woke her at 3:00 a.m. and she heard the voice of her husband's drunken lover, she didn't appreciate it.

At that time Melissa and I owned property on a lake in the Tennessee Valley, where we planned to retire together. During the Christmas break, Melissa and I were sorting some of our snapshots, and she began to tear up when she came across some photos of the Tennessee property. I knew that she was thinking that our dream of a pleasant and peaceful retirement together might fall apart if my relationship with Antwon kept interfering. Would we be able to hold our marriage together into retirement? By the time Melissa picked up Antwon's drunken phone call, we had suffered through almost two years of my intense emotional reactions to Antwon's behaviors.

No matter how much it hurt him and upset me, I decided it was time to end the relationship with Antwon. By then I had already met Vern, a man my own age who interested me. I had no idea whether my relationship with Vern would go anywhere, but he embodied the fact that I had other options for continuing my bisexual life. I had to lead my bisexual life in a way that was not so destructive to Melissa or to me.

Breaking up is never easy. Antwon, like most alcoholics, denied his pattern of binge drinking. But we parted respectfully.

By Valentine's Day, Melissa was feeling secure again, and wrote on her annual Valentine's card to me: "I'm so glad that we're [no longer] talking of going our separate ways.... I feel so much better when I know that there is still room for me, and for our relationship, in our lives. I want to grow old with you. This has been a happy Valentine's Day and I hope it will stay that way. You have been and always will be the most important person in my life... I sincerely hope we can make it work. Love always, Melissa."

Some years later, Antwon called, and I went to see him. He was now in regular counseling with a mental health worker, had been diagnosed as bipolar, and was responding well to psychotropic drugs monitored by the local mental health center. He believed his drinking had been a form of self-medicating, a way of handling his bipolar disorder.

Knowing this made Anton's behaviors more understandable. I'm grateful we could end our relationship without acrimony.

CHAPTER 22
BOUNDARIES AND BALANCE

Rules, agreements, and clear boundaries helped Melissa and me deal with my bisexual exploration and the rebuilding of trust in our second marriage. One agreement was both helpful and amusing: we were "monogamous" about watching modern dance performances!

Melissa and I felt that it would be good to have some regular but special event that we pursued only with each other. We chose modern dance partly because we are both enthusiasts, but also because it is sensuous and beautiful and has the power to move us. Invariably, as we sit together watching a beautiful performance, one of us will hold the other's hand or put an arm around the other. The types of choreography and music we resonate with are amazingly similar.

Paradoxically, modern dance provided a space where Melissa became more acquainted with the gay world. It became obvious to both of us at dance performances that much of the audience consisted of gay male couples. Attending the "Dance for Life" benefit for agencies dealing with HIV/AIDS in Chicago has become an important annual ritual for Melissa and me. It is one of the few places where my involvement in the gay community enters the time I share with Melissa. Because she is a nurse and has worked intensively with HIV-infected children, she shares in the grief the epidemic has caused.

Over the years, it has become clear us that outside friendships will never replace or destroy our marriage. Monogamy in all its forms seems less important.

Melissa has a passionate interest in figure skating, and we enjoy seeing competitive events together. She is much more knowledgeable than I about the rules of scoring and about past and current stars. She has gone to several national and international competitions with her close friend Lois. The fact that Melissa sometimes attends figure skating events with her friend does not seem to diminish the enjoyment Melissa and I have when we go together.

Very early in our relationship we recognized that, although the visual arts, drama, and opera are important to me, they are of little interest to Melissa. Sometimes I go to the art museum or to a play alone. But I also enjoy going with some of my friends, typically with friends that Melissa does not share. I frequently go to plays with a straight married couple from our church whose business involves drama; their comments afterward increase my understanding of the play.

Other arts-based friendships include those with a professional artist-photographer who was a respondent in one of my research projects, a former student who climbed mountains as a photographer for National Geographic, and a young relative who plans to become an artist.

The freedom both Melissa and I feel to pursue our own interests enhances our relationship, in that it allows each of us to be fully who we are rather than becoming clones of each other.

~ ~ ~

For years I have been active in the Unitarian Universalist church in our area. Although the majority of our church members are straight, several LBGT members have held leadership positions. A lesbian member who regularly attended services with her partner was elected President of the congregation. Another was a board member. And I was the leader of the major adult education program and one of the regular teachers for the teenage Sunday school class.

A few years after my retirement, after surveying the

area, I recognized that there was no place in the south suburbs, other than bars, for LBGT people to socialize. I proposed that our congregation provide a safe space. In 2007 the church supported my initiating the Rainbow Café, a regular meeting for les-bi-gay-trans persons. The Rainbow Café has been meeting in our church social room ever since. Some of those who attended were already members of our Unitarian Universalist church, but most were not. Although the meetings are purely social with no intent to promote our church, several of the regular Rainbow participants sensed the level of acceptance of this congregation and became members themselves.

After I retired from the University, this congregation remained one of my most important support systems. In 2009 the church searched for a new minister and chose a black man who was openly "same gender loving," (a phrase many African Americans prefer to "gay").

My intense involvement in the local church reflects the fact that I still consider ministry my vocation. But this church has also become one of my most important support groups, a setting where I can be unguarded about my bisexual life.

~ ~ ~

Melissa and Lois made a life-changing trip together in 1999. They were still busy running their pediatric home care business, but they had a special invitation to go to Africa as managed care consultants for Ambassador to Ambassador, a program directed by Anne Eisenhower, daughter of the former president. Melissa and Lois both became passionately interested in helping HIV-infected orphans who had survived the AIDS epidemic in Africa. Together they initiated projects in South Africa, Kenya, and Tanzania. Melissa spent many weekends at Lois's home planning and executing projects to fund their work in Africa. At last Melissa had a valued friendship that balanced my outside life. We were both grateful. A new pattern began: Melissa traveled with her close friend while I did the same with mine.

While visiting an orphanage in South Africa, Lois and Melissa decided to help build a school there. About two years later I traveled with them to celebrate the completion of the first phase of the school. I will never forget the day we spent with a dedicated woman social worker who visited four child-led families in Soweto – families in which both parents had died in the AIDS epidemic. The children were surviving because the social worker was supporting the oldest child in taking on the tasks of parenting. It was a testimony to how resilient children can be when given emotional support and teaching.

Melissa, Lois and I then flew on to tour parts of Kenya and Tanzania. The trip deepened my commitment to AIDS work in the US and increased two of my convictions: that thoughtful and truly collaborative interventions in desperate situations can be effective, and that secular ministries are as much a part of sacred work as are church-related ministries.

CHAPTER 23
REACHING INWARD

"In loneliness, when one is tempted to reach outward overmuch, it's time to reach inward."
- Chris Glaser, Uncommon Calling

One way Melissa and I learned to reach out, especially when we first moved to a new area and were missing old friends, was to initiate a regularly-meeting personal growth group in which we could develop trust and openness. The spirituality groups we formed at the beginning of our Midwestern years and early in our Chicago years are examples.

In about 1995, a group of counselors in our area started a clinical support group consisting of nine members with different theoretical orientations. Two decades later, seven members of the group continue to meet every other week, sharing our personal struggles and joys whether or not they affect our clinical work. In many ways the group has become our adult family.

I appreciated the need for support around me fairly early in my adult life; it took me a bit longer to fully appreciate the value of reaching inward in times of loneliness. Locating places in which I could be at peace, either alone or with an intimate friend, became a part of my spiritual discipline. My childhood hikes to the Old Fort, sitting by the fishing pond without baiting my hook, walking in the hills gathering flowers with my German friend, and strolling through wooded areas with Melissa: these places were "stepping stones – one safe haven after another across the rapids," as Judith Barrington wrote in *Lifesaving: A Memoir*.

Poetry has been another aid to my inner work. Although I rarely write poetry for publication, I love reading it aloud and attending readings, especially by the poets themselves. The Robert Bly "Great Mother" conferences were crucial to my development of a deep appreciation for the power of writing in images, a central feature of poetry.

Classical music, especially from the Romantic to early modern periods, has been very important to my becoming grounded in my emotions. The best situation is a live orchestral performance, sitting beside Melissa. Sometimes I listen to recorded music that I've chosen because of the mood or feeling it conveys.

What is most important for me is to step outside the constant rush of life and the external bombardment of stimuli, and to get in tune with my own bodily experience and emotions.

I am especially open to the spiritual when I am close to nature and in a community of people I have learned to trust. In 1997 I was attending a "Great Mother/New Father" conference on a heavily wooded campground on a lake in Maine – an annual event initiated by poet Robert Bly. About 25 of the 80 or so people attending knew me from previous conferences and from a monthly in-house publication in which we share essays, poems, and personal reflections. I felt very trusting and comfortable with this group.

It was a beautiful summer day. For several successive afternoons, Mel Chartrand and Shirley Jesmer, a married couple who are licensed therapists and members of the Ojibwa nation, had led our meditations. Forty or fifty of us had chosen to learn a new form of breathwork and meditation. We sat in a circle facing a huge fieldstone fireplace in a quiet, dimly-lit barn. After we completed the breathing exercises, Mel instructed us, "Return to normal breathing now, but follow your own visual fantasies. Stay in touch with your body feelings, as well as the images that emerge in your fantasies."

My fantasies encouraged me to leave the lodge and walk slowly down the grassy hill toward the lake. As I was approaching the shore, I saw several empty kayaks lying on the dock. I put on a safety vest, slid a kayak into the water, pulled it even to the dock, laid a paddle across the kayak, and carefully climbed in. The water was very calm, so it was easy to glide quietly out into the lake and paddle around an island a quarter of a mile away. From there, I could no longer see the camp or any of the people attending the conference. I felt happy to be at one with nature – alone, yet conscious of friends there I could trust.

Some time passed as I continued to paddle, seeing only calm water and low-lying clouds near the horizon. I noticed that one of the clouds on the horizon gently began to grow. Upward and upward, billowing and white, tall as an enormous thundercloud – the change was surreal and quite beautiful. I couldn't take my eyes off this amazing cloud, and yet I was aware of the calmness around me. I felt very much connected to all that is.

I sensed in my body that the cloud was a warm and loving "other." I felt love emanating from this huge and dreamlike cloud, love flowing toward me. Then I heard a voice – not an actual sound, not something that could be recorded – but a distinct and clear voice. It was my father's voice.

My father has been dead for twenty years; for several years he spoke to me in dreams, yet this is no dream.

I felt calm, knowing that I was safe on the lake and that a supportive community was back on shore meditating.

A rich belly laugh roared from the cloud! It was the warm laughter of my father's loving voice. In my dreams I had heard, with a touch of sadness, his wishes for me and the assurance of his love for me. But I had forgotten his wonderful laugh. I realized Dad was telling me, "Don't worry yourself for me – and don't remember me with longing or sadness. Instead, remember my laugh."

For reasons I still do not understand, I had delayed coming out to my family as bisexual until after Dad died. Now, twenty-five years after his death, I had this experience of closeness to him, almost as if he'd come back to assure me,

"I'm OK with you, Dave. I know you're bisexual, and that's OK with me."

This was one of the most moving mystical experiences I have had. I see no need to explain it. I'm simply glad that I was open to the experience. It brought joy to my heart – not just my father's joy, but the joy of my creation. I was created bisexual, and that is the Divine plan for me. My Dad approves. I rejoice in ALL creation.

~ ~ ~

Nature, poetry, music, visual arts, and simply being in silence each facilitate my being open to the Mystery. These practices reduce my fear of differences of thought or of changing boundaries. When I experiment with being more generous and more loving, I become more and more convinced that the opposite of love is not hate, but fear.

My hunch is that almost all rejection of differences is fear-based. The rejection of Muslims by Christian dogmatists, the rejection of gays by defenders of traditional masculine superiority, the rejection of the equality of women – all these are fear-based. The spiritual questions that continue to interest me center around how to embrace nature and other humans in love and praise, and yet not seek false assurance. Fearless love is an open and growing process. Creeds and dogma do not help us grow into love and away from fear. They lack the tentativeness and the playfulness that characterize "childlike faith" as Jesus described it. In contrast love, like myth and poetry and art, is fertilized by playfulness.

CHAPTER 24
INDIA LONGER AND DEEPER

When I mail a fistful of letters to institutions spread over many hundreds of miles, I imagine myself as a sower of seeds. I've done this several times in my life, beginning with my applications to many liberal arts colleges in 1955; later with my seeking the right place to minister as a counselor and teacher in 1968; and this time, in 2000, as I searched for a place to connect more deeply with day-to-day life in India.

I had become convinced, based on my previous experience in Denmark, that the best way to understand a culture is to take a job and live in the culture for a time. I was able to arrange my teaching schedule at Governors State so that I could spend four months teaching abroad.

My hope was to return to India. the country in which my mother had wanted to serve as a missionary and which I had explored ten years before. I accepted an offer to teach for one term at Visva-Bharati University in the state of West Bengal. The University has a liberal arts college with a counseling program and a strong emphasis on East/West dialogue. One of my mother's heroes, Rabindranath Tagore, had founded the college. [12] Tagore, Gandhi's mentor, was not only one of India's greatest authors, but also was a lover and practitioner of both music and painting.

As I had done decades before in Denmark, I would work in culture I had fallen in love with. But this would be different in two important ways: I would be working in a non-Western culture, and Melissa would not be going with me.

Melissa and Lois were very much occupied with their

pediatric home care agency. In spite of her lack of interest in India, Melissa supported my going and offered to come for a few weeks in the middle of my stay.

The college arranged for me to live in a small inn within bicycling distance from the campus. My apartment consisted of two large rooms on the second floor, with lovely views of the rural surroundings. The inn provided two meals a day.

I was named a University Professor there, which meant I could teach in classes in any department. Soon after I arrived, I circulated a letter to all faculty listing about twenty topics on which I would be willing to teach as a guest in their class. Classes met for three-hour periods, so my idea was that during the first hour and a half, I would present the viewpoint of an American on a particular subject. During the second half of the class, the students and professor could present an Indian perspective on the same subject.

The response delighted me. I was invited to join a variety of courses, including a physical education class (focusing on competition from the perspectives of the two cultures) and a series of classes in the social work department (comparing Eastern and Western styles of interventions in counseling). It was a wonderful way to learn more about the culture.

Dr. Sherry Joseph, a social psychologist and fellow faculty member, lived nearby with his wife Linu and their precocious preschool daughter Annette, who loved showing off her understanding of English. We became good friends. Several other local faculty members as well as a temporary professor from Germany were both friendly and supportive.

When Melissa joined me halfway through my stay, I introduced her to the two Indian families with whom I'd grown closest. We also spent the two or three weeks in which I had no teaching responsibilities visiting some of the Himalayan mountain range, which I found inspiring. We traveled by train, bus, and a car with a professional driver into the Darjeeling region, where we saw the range that includes Mt. Everest.

It was wonderful being with Melissa again and showing her the life I was leading there. Since she was familiar with third world countries, she adjusted easily to the culture. The heat and humidity were hard for her (whether in Africa or India), so the trip to the Himalayas was a relief.

Some weeks after Melissa returned to the US, I traveled alone by train to Varanasi (Benares), a city on the banks of the Ganges. It is one of the oldest continually-inhabited cities in the world and is regarded as holy by Hindus, Buddhists, and Jains. I spent hours meditating on the banks and watched an extended family throughout much of a day as they cremated an elder on a funeral pyre. The undisguised facing of death seemed more healthy than our cosmeticized viewing of the body in funeral homes. In nearby Sarnath I visited the deer park where Gautama Buddha gave his first sermon, one of the four pilgrimage sites related to the Buddha's life. Since Buddhism has profoundly influenced my own spirituality, walking in the areas he walked helped me feel more grounded in this perspective.

On a separate trip, I visited Bodh Gaya, a small tourist city considered the most important of the Buddhist pilgrimage sites. It is there, under a huge tree, that the Buddha is believed to have attained enlightenment. A large tree grows there today. Some say that it is the very tree under which the Buddha sat; others say that it is descended from that tree. Believers from almost every nation with a large Buddhist population have built temples in this village.

I was meditatively strolling from temple to temple when I sensed that a tall Buddhist monk in his bright orange robe was gazing at me. There were many such monks, but this man, probably in his forties, seemed fixed on me. I continued to stroll, occasionally making eye contact, and he followed me. Eventually I turned to face him and walked slowly toward him, gently smiling. I greeted him with the palms-together gesture and word "Namaste" and asked if he spoke English, but he did not even understand my question. For an hour or more we strolled together, entering various temples. I decided to buy some fruit, bread, and other food and gestured for him to follow me as I walked into the market area. We selected some things together and walked back to the small inn where I was staying. We ate silently in my bedroom.

I needed a nap, and there was a bed and a cot in the room. I gestured that I wanted to sleep and that he was welcome to nap as well. He chose to sit on the cot, although I think he lay down when he saw me do so. We were remarkably relaxed being together, even though it was perfectly quiet most of the time. It is very rare, in my experience, to have such relaxed silence with a new acquaintance. I believe each of us sensed that the other had also come to Bodh Gaya as part of a personal pilgrimage, that we knew our lives and pilgrimages were rather different, but that a deep respect for each other and each other's path was present. It wasn't important to be able to communicate in words, since the common ground of our lives was known and respected.

Somehow we managed to convey to each other that we wanted to meet again and have another meal together. The next day I led him to a local restaurant. The menu was in many languages, and he was able to point to what he wanted to order. Despite street noise and others chatting in the restaurant, all was quiet between us. Again I loved and honored the silence, feeling very much connected with him, with this town of temples, and with the spirit of the Buddha. He wrote out his name, Tenzin Uyinra, from Nyingmap monastery in Tibet. Perhaps he was inviting me to visit there. I gave him my calling card with my Illinois address, although I knew he couldn't read it and that I probably would never hear from him again.

The next day Tenzin came to my room in the morning. We knew we would both be leaving Bodh Gaya that day. I would take a taxi to the train, and he would ride with me to the train station and go on his own way from there. When we parted, my inclination was to give him a warm hug, but I suspected that physical contact would be awkward for him. I knew, and I'm sure he knew, that there was no way to continue to be in touch through any written words. Ours was a relationship without words. We gazed into each other's eyes for a long time. Eventually, we each placed our hands in the traditional prayer position, gently bowed to each other, and uttered together a caring "Namaste." We parted from each other with that holy gesture and words meaning "I honor the god within you."

Back at Visva-Bharati one sunny afternoon, a man I'd met previously spotted me on campus and crossed over the quad to converse with me. Marcus was from the US, but he had lived for several years in India. He said, "I had a feeling you might be interested in visiting the Mother House of Mother Theresa in Calcutta while you're living here."

"You're right, I would like to go there," I responded, "but I think it would feel awkward just to tour the house."

"True. But I've been doing volunteer work there a few days a month for some time now. Would you considering joining me?"

"I don't want to make a regular commitment," I answered. "I use my weekends to see other areas of West

Bengal. But could I go with you for just one day that you're volunteering?" He assured me he could arrange it.

Seldom have I been involved in working for a charity where my presence was so effectively utilized. On my arrival I was led to three other male volunteers in a basement area where several warm water showers hung from the ceiling pipes. The volunteers were showering the homeless men who had been brought to the center off the streets.

One of the volunteers showed me to a bunk area on the same floor and gestured toward a particular man. I walked over to this smelly, emaciated Indian man, awake on the cot where he'd apparently spent the night. I motioned for him to follow me. As he started to get up I could see he was unstable; I spontaneously put an arm around his waist, and he placed his arm across my shoulders. As I assisted him to the shower area, I was conscious that he was trusting an absolute stranger who didn't speak his language. I helped him strip off the filthy clothes he was wearing. Then, steadying him in the warm shower water, I lathered his whole body and then rinsed him down. He seemed grateful to be bathed and showed no self-consciousness about my physical contact with him. Perhaps he could sense that it was caring and nurturing.

Another volunteer joined us, and together we toweled this homeless man down. I walked him back to his cot, on which clean clothes had been placed, and helped him put them on. As I was about to leave him, I placed my hands in the "Namaste" gesture, and he responded in kind. Once again I was awakened to the power of nonverbal communication when there is honest respect between two people.

I repeated a similar process with three or four other men, until we volunteers had showered them all. Then I took up another task, carrying freshly washed laundry up to the roof and laying it out to dry in the hot Indian sunshine.

~ ~ ~

In my last weeks in Asia I traveled again to the Himalayas. This time I arranged a flight in a small two-propeller plane. I joined about six others to get a close view of Mt. Everest. So many spiritual adventures were coming to an end, but I wanted to take my leave in the beauty of nature. I traveled on into Nepal, first to Kathmandu and then into the area surrounding Pokhara, a place of awesome beauty. There I hiked quietly with a guide who knew the trails and respected the silence. The climax of my trip, at the very end of my time in Nepal, was with a busload of tourists staying overnight high in the Himalayas and rising early to watch the sunrise shining on the face of Mt. Everest.

> Breathless I stopped
> In front is love
> Living ecstasy
> Darkness vanished
> Light filled the land
> Smiled in tears
> It kissed my soul
>
> - From Cheryl Joy Amarga, "Sunrise Delight"

CHAPTER 25
NEW PATHS

For eighteen years Melissa and I had not had much free time together. The pediatric home health care organization that she co-managed was amazingly successful; teaching and counseling occupied much of my own time. The remainder I devoted to my church life, my gay life, and my writing (publishing my second book in 1993 and beginning a book on spirituality and counseling).

In 2002, I was offered a buyout from the State University System, which wanted long-tenured faculty to retire early to reduce the state's expenditures on salaries. The scene that followed was a familiar one: Melissa and I were sitting at the kitchen table discussing plans. I had loved my job, but I was tired of teaching certain courses.

"What really excites you, in the way of work?" Melissa asked me.

I answered without hesitation: "The course that excites me most is my new one in spirituality and counseling. It's in the schedule for this coming summer, but if I accept a retirement package they'd like me to quit before then. I'd miss teaching the group counseling courses, but I could use my group skills in some settings at church."

"What about your private practice?"

"I enjoy that, but I wouldn't mind tapering it off – finishing with my present clients but only taking new ones if they're particularly interesting, like gay couples and mixed orientation marriages."

Melissa paused. "I'm afraid if you're not working, you'll get bored and want to travel a lot, and I'm not ready to retire for several years yet."

"Well, besides teaching the class, I want to finish my book on spirituality and counseling. Teaching the class gives me a chance to test out the experiential exercises I plan to put in the book. So a big hunk of my time would go into that. And I'd love to do some more traveling."

"I love to travel too. So make a list of the countries you want to go to, and I'll mark the ones I want you to save for me. The others you can do with whoever before I retire."

I accepted the early retirement package with the provision that I would still teach the scheduled course in spirituality and counseling.

So my retirement years began in stages. In 2002 I ended 34 years of teaching and doing research, freeing me to travel. With four different gay men, I visited Russia, the Czech Republic, Peru, and Japan.

The following year I reduced my private practice, focusing on my writing. My third book, the one on spirituality and counseling, was published in 2008. I continued other writing, but ended my clinical work in 2009.

My relationship with Michael intensified the year after I retired. We discovered that each of us had been going regularly to the George Bernard Shaw Festival in Ontario. The idea of going together and sharing a room at a gay B&B appealed to both of us, both financially and sexually. Michael and I began traveling together more frequently. The experience was so enjoyable that we went to Montreal the following summer (2004) for the GALA, a festival of gay and lesbian choruses. Michael, who sang with his city's gay men's chorus, would be performing with them. We started planning regular trips together, and I began to think of him as my lover.

The following year we went to the Shaw Festival, to Epcot Center in Orlando, and to Japan with a remarkable three-week Elderhostel trip. Although I did most of the planning, Michael was the skillful navigator after we embarked. These roles became the rule for the many trips that have followed.

Each year we spent time at each other's homes, attended the Shaw Festival, and took one major trip together, visiting another country, an important archeological site, or an artists' community such as Saugatuck, Michigan. I enjoyed learning from Michael about drama and archeology, and Michael joined me in exploring modern art.

Being together all the time on these long trips and sharing a room and often a bed in a B&B made our relationship more intimate. We have become caring and cooperative partners in travel – and that has extended to more and more sharing of our lives.

I don't remember on which trip it occurred, but as our relationship deepened Michael and I became clearer in letting each other know what each wanted from the other. After a meal with several other couples, when Michael and I were alone in our B&B bedroom, Michael said, "When we're together and we get to talking with other couples, I wish you wouldn't bring up your kids. It invariably leads to your having to explain about your being married. Sometimes people may think that your marriage is in the past, since they sense that we are a couple. But usually you have to explain about your agreements with Melissa and your bisexuality."

"But you know all that. It's not something I hide from you," I responded, trying to understand what bothered him.

"Of course I do. And I think it's remarkable that you and Melissa have worked this out. You know I don't want to do anything that gets in the way of your marriage. But when I'm with you in these social settings, I want people to see us as a couple. I'd like it if they saw just you and me – if they just thought of us as gay friends, or a gay couple, and didn't get distracted trying to deal with your marriage!"

I suddenly realized what he meant. It was partly that he, like Melissa, needed boundaries. But the purpose wasn't to protect him. He wanted the two of us to remain the focus so we could be treated simply as a gay couple, not as part of a complex and confusing arrangement.

After I understood, I actually enjoyed it. To let people assume I'm gay – to fully affirm my gay side – shouldn't be hard, since when I'm with Melissa most of the time people assume I'm straight.

After about four years of my regularly visiting or traveling with Michael, Melissa had become quite comfortable with our relationship. She'd often comment as I was leaving, "Say hi to Michael," or "Give him my good wishes."

Michael and I traveled together many times throughout the period of our becoming a steady couple. Not only did our relationship prosper, so did Elderhostel's tour business, as well as that of several bed and breakfasts!

We traveled to the home of my first gay lover Ben and his Malaysian partner Omar. It was especially enjoyable to visit them and go out to dinner as two gay couples. When I had first entered the gay scene, I didn't even know gay couples existed! And those I got to know a decade or more later often did not exist in a public way. But here we were, two gay couples in Arizona, a conservative southwestern state, going to restaurants together.

I'm not sure whether traveling together or living together is the more stringent test of whether a relationship can work. But it has become clear that my relationship with Michael works remarkably well. We are not exclusive in our gay sexual contacts, but each of us consistently lets the other know of any involvements that we've had between our times together. In terms of values, Michael and I are quite similar. And thanks to his seeking therapeutic help, Michael is very comfortable about being gay, although he waited until retirement to be open about it. We are both direct and honest in our communication with each other and have made serious efforts to respect each other's personality and life situation. If Michael were to find a gay partner with whom he wanted to have a primary relationship, I would not stand in the way. But at this stage in life it seems unlikely to happen. I'm reasonably sure we will be together till death us do part.

~ ~ ~

One summer afternoon, a widowed man phoned me about counseling for his fifteen-year-old son, who he feared might be gay. The father wanted to meet with me alone before I saw his son. "If I see you alone first," I told the father, "it's likely to be harder for me to develop a connection with your son. He might feel that you'd already given me a negative impression of him."

They came together for the first session. My counseling room was filled with old farm tools that whispered messages from my father's and grandfather's era and seemed to put this rural father more at ease. The father seemed intensely involved with his son. The boy's mother had died recently, leaving only the two of them. The father, a Catholic from Italy, had recently learned that his son had attended a gay youth group. He hoped I would be able to change the boy. But underneath his anger I sensed a mixture of strong connection with the son and fear about the son's future if he were gay. I used that session to develop empathy with both men, without taking sides on the gay issue.

For the second session, I met with the son alone. Almost immediately, he told me that he was gay. With palpable fear and on the edge of tears, he confessed, "I haven't told my dad yet. I'm so scared he's going to throw me out of the house if he finds out. I've lost my mother. I don't have any brothers or sisters. I couldn't bear it if I lost Dad."

I did not disclose my own bisexuality to the son; to do so would have created a positive bond between us, but it would have been risky, as the son might have used the information to one-up his father, destroying my authority in the father's eyes. But it was clear that I respected the young man's age-appropriate longing for more independence and his need for peer relationships. The son also realized that I had knowledge of the gay community and that I did not reject gays or him.

For the third session, I met alone with the father. Two moral or spiritual issues were motivating him: his view that homosexual behavior would be a sinful or at least a dangerous direction for his son, and his love and responsibility as a father. When there was enough rapport, I asked him, "What is a Christian father's responsibility to his son?"

After more listening and reflecting, I reminded the father that although Jesus tells his disciples that following him may "lead son away from father" (Matthew 10:34-36; Luke 12:51-53), nowhere in the gospels does Jesus give permission for a father to abandon his son. My intent was to block the father from acting out in anger and rejecting the young man. Of course it was not my responsibility to engage the father in a discussion about my own theology or ethics. I did see it as important to challenge him, and to do so within *his own* religious and ethical system. Despite the father's fear and anger, he was part of a deep Christian tradition that emphasized the Father God's love for his Son (Matthew 10:34-36; 4:11) and the good father's rejoicing at the return of the wayward son (Luke 15:11-32).

Fortunately, the bond between this particular father and son was strong.

The father resonated deeply with his religious duty. He realized that he did not want the homosexual issue to sever the bonds between him and his son. I helped the man express directly that he would not want his son to leave until he was mature enough. And the father began to trust me enough to let me point out some of his misperceptions about the dangers of gay culture.

CHAPTER 26
BEYOND JEALOUSY

When my relationship with Michael had become steady, Melissa and I negotiated times when it would be acceptable for me to invite Michael to our home when Melissa would be on a trip with Lois or staying at Lois's home.

Now that Melissa no longer fears that I will leave her, it seems less important to her to protect our space. This became clear one day when I was preparing for Michael to visit. Melissa was in our bedroom packing for a trip with Lois. I went to the linen closet to get sheets to make up the bed for Michael; on previous visits, he had always slept in the guest room, not in the master bedroom that Melissa and I use.

"You know," Melissa said, "you don't have to do that. It's OK if you and Michael want to use the double bed. It's more comfortable."

Surprised, I asked, "Are you sure?"

"Yes," she said. "It just doesn't seem to be an issue any more."

I was grateful for her generosity and her lack of jealousy. I let her know how lucky I felt to have her as a partner.

Recently, after reviewing some notes we had made before our remarriage ceremony, I asked Melissa how she felt now about being primary in my life. She said she felt that she was closer to being primary now. She believed it was partly due to my being older and less interested in wandering and experience-seeking, but it was also because of my relationship with Michael. I agreed. Michael has never expected to be co-equal to Melissa in my relationship with him. He has never had a partner who was committed primarily to him, and he doesn't expect that from me since he is totally respectful of my marriage to Melissa.

Of course, there are still boundaries. Melissa and I try to coordinate our trips so both of us can go our separate ways. And we make time for the things we love doing together when we are both at home or on a trip together. But clearly Melissa has grown beyond jealousy. This is a quality that is hard for most people in our culture to understand. In college classes where I've talked about our unusual marriage, women are the most likely to express amazement that Melissa no longer sees jealousy as the sign of love. Men, who tend to be less committed to monogamy, are more likely to say nothing during the class, but they often come up to me afterward and confide that they are envious.

Never before in my life have I felt so satisfied on both sides (in my heterosexuality and my homosexuality) and so comfortable about handling both relationships simultaneously. There is little conflict or anxiety involved. Both Michael and Melissa are relaxed and comfortable about the other's role in my life. This is a wonderful time for me – probably the most satisfying period I've had since I first recognized my bisexuality.

Michael and I also have direct communication and agreements. We are free to have outside involvements, but we have always told each other if we have had any contact that could have even the slightest risk of transmitting STDs. We've done this out of respect and because we want to protect each other's health. Even safe sex is, actually, only saf*er* sex. It is not foolproof.

Michael and I find it relatively easy to speak honestly to each other about such incidents, partly because neither one of us is particularly jealous. Given any new information about each other's recent sex life, we can make whatever decisions we feel comfortable with concerning what sex we'll have together. We both get tested for STDs regularly, and we certainly have done so after any encounter with another gay man outside our relationship. I do not engage in sex with either of my regular partners, Melissa or Michael, until I have test results and know that it's safe.

One of the wonderful things about communication with both of my partners is that we are absolutely honest about anything that could affect the other. And the relationships are secure enough that we know that the truth won't separate us. Even if we learn something that doesn't make us happy, we will find a way to work it through.

Michael has been forthright in sharing his own interests in looking elsewhere, enjoying seeing other bodies in the shower at the YMCA, and so on. He has commented that encounters in the Y are safer than in the woods! But once I called him to tell him about something that happened in the woods.

"I have two things I want to tell you about," I said. "One story is about something I'm proud of – I suppose you could call it a generous thing I've done. The other is more selfish. I guess I'll tell the selfish one first."

"Good news and bad news. Yeah, tell the bad news first," Michael responded.

"Well, yesterday I drove to the forest preserve to walk. As I got out of my car in the parking lot, a man in another car called over to me asking 'What kind of car is that?'"

Jake, the man who called to me, was also married, and I told Michael that the encounter had moved from conversation to driving together to a safe place where we could have a sexual experience.

Michael laughed comfortably, and then said, "I guess

we're all cut from the same cloth." He simply meant that like most men who are honest about it, both of us have our eyes open and enjoy seeing people who are sexually attractive to us – enjoying eye candy, as the saying goes.

He listened empathetically to my story. I told him that Jake and I had exchanged phone numbers. "But I have been thinking that it's not a good idea to let the relationship continue in a sexual way. He's 22 years younger than I. From what he told me, I think Jake really needs to focus on finding someone with whom he can have a more equal relationship. I told him that I have a commitment to you, Michael, and after all, how many lovers can one man manage?"

Again Michael laughed, but I made it clear that having two lovers is as complicated as I want my life to be.

"So," I continued, "if he should call me, I would probably see him once in some setting where we can talk, but where it won't become sexual. I don't want him to think I'm rejecting him as a person, so I would want to tell him why I don't think a continued relationship would be good for either of us."

"So what was the 'good news'?" Michael asked. Relieved that Michael had taken my adventure so well, I told him about the other remarkable incident.

I had gone with friends to see Phil Donahue's movie *Body of War*. It's about a young man who served in Iraq, was shot in the spine just below the neck, and became paralyzed from the upper chest down. I don't think I have ever seen a movie where I felt as much empathy and new understanding of what it's like to lose the power to move autonomously – to have your own body refuse to do what you want it to do, and to have to depend on others for help so much of the time. When the movie ended, I walked out of the dark theater and into the men's restroom. As I was about to walk out of the restroom, a young man in a motorized wheelchair entered. He said, in the difficult-to-understand slurred speech of someone who's lost muscle control, "Will you hel' me?"

Surprised, but willing to try to help, I responded, "Yes, I'll help you. What do you need?" He had soiled himself and needed to clean up. We went into the accessible stall and I helped him undress.

We told each other our names; at first I thought his was Al, but I finally realized it was Matt. He was calm and patient about my difficulties in understanding him, in spite of the situation. He kept apologizing and asked me, "How much can I pay you for helping?"

"You don't need to pay me," I said. "I wanted to help. That's what we're here for, to help each other."

I washed his pants and underpants at the sink. Meanwhile a few other men came into the restroom. One of them stopped to asked me if he could be of help. I asked him to do the drying using one of the two hand-dryers.

As we worked, Matt asked me if he could take me out to dinner. I thanked him and said that if I hadn't had other plans, I would have been glad to go to dinner with him. But it was my daughter's birthday, and she and my wife were waiting for me at a restaurant. Then another thought came to me. "Matt, do you know you've already given me a lot? You've helped me realize how lucky I am to be able to walk and to move freely, and that I shouldn't take that for granted." The man drying the pants said, "He's right, Matt." I wished I had been free to go to dinner and get to know Matt better. The three of us left the men's room together.

It struck me as more than coincidence that just after feeling empathy for the paraplegic soldier in the movie, I had the chance to try out what I had learned in a real-life situation. But when all was done, as well as it could be done, I felt close to Matt. I felt thankful for the ability to show deep caring through physical contact – for the sense that something very real and concrete had been given.

I took the escalator down several flights to head to the restaurant. I got out my cell phone, called two people I love very much, my wife and my daughter, and explained what had happened.

When I finished telling my story to Michael on the phone, I thanked him for listening so non-judgmentally.

There are so many kinds of love. The adventure with Jake was one of lust – but it was also deeply respectful and surprisingly personal. To think of it as an impersonal act just because I had not known him until that day is as false as it would be to think of my interaction with Matt as impersonal.

I had felt both caring and admiration for Matt. I had given and received sexual love with Jake. And I was so grateful to be able to open and honest with Michael and to know he gave me love in his listening and in his laughter.

So here I was, bathed in two days of love. The encounter in the forest with Jake. Then the movie, and the caring relationship with Matt. Then time with my wife and daughter. And now the phone call with Michael.

How different these concrete experiences in love were, on those two special days, compared to the abstract rules and expectations that society has invented. How did American culture get the idea that love emerges only in a relationship between one man and one woman? Although there is much to be criticized about the Old Testament standard for marital love – one man with several wives and concubines – at least it allowed the family to know a variety of loves. And although by Jesus's time the standard for marriage had changed, his recorded words show no judgment toward the older pattern, although he knew the Hebrew scriptures well, and was not reluctant to disagree with them.[13]

What Jesus did criticize was men divorcing – failing to live out the covenants they had made to support and care for their wives. A divorced woman in those days was usually doomed to live in poverty, rejected by society.

As far as we know, Jesus said nothing about love between two men or two women. The nature of marriage has changed across many cultures and over many centuries. But the idea that the Bible stands for only heterosexual monogamy but allows divorce is based on ignorance of the Bible.

~ ~ ~

One morning, as we lay in bed together, I said to Melissa, "I'm working on the part of my memoir where I'm writing about Michael. I've been trying to think, what makes it different? It seems so much easier for you to handle my relationship with Michael than it was with previous relationships."

Melissa instantly ticked off a series of reasons: "Michael is close to your own age. He doesn't telephone all the time. You do most of your communicating on email – so I don't have to hear the phone ring and possibly answer it and deal directly with him. Michael doesn't live right here in Chicago area. He isn't so needy. You don't have to worry about him. Of course you are concerned about his health right now. But he takes care of himself – he isn't dependent on you."

Melissa went on to compare Michael to Antwon. She avoids using his name. "In contrast to when you were seeing 'that young squirt,' you don't bring Michael up all the time. Occasionally you need to check out dates with me: would it work if you and Michael went on such and such trip? But it isn't like you're preoccupied with him and thinking or talking about him doesn't constantly interrupt our time together."

I responded to Melissa's analysis by mentioning a song

I'd heard at a concert the other day. It was an old Irish song, and each verse was followed by a two-line refrain:

"And I still haven't found what I long for.
No, I still haven't found what I long for."

I noted that when I was involved with the affair with "that young squirt" back in 1991, and for many years before that, I felt that I still hadn't found what I longed for. But I rarely feel that now. "I am much more centered," I said. I feel this not only in my gay relationships, but when I'm with younger men who want me to be a substitute father or a mentor.

The obvious fact that I've grown older is part of it. Sexual desire is not so central as it was when I was younger. That's true for both Melissa and me, and for Michael and me.

There are two other factors I would add: Michael has been a friend much longer than he was a lover, and as strong as the relationship was and is, it did not come from neediness or desperation. And Melissa now has a deep friendship outside of our marriage; in some ways her friendship with Lois balances my relationship with Michael. Neither Melissa nor Lois is bisexual or lesbian; their relationship is not sexual. But their friendship and work relationship is very involving and time-consuming, and meets their mutual needs. It provides a good balance.

In the more than fifty years that Melissa and I have sustained our committed love, we have learned to love each other for wonderful qualities and for personality quirks and idiosyncrasies. She has come to a very deep acceptance of my bisexuality as who I am. Her acceptance reverberates with the kind of unconditional love I felt from my mother in childhood. And just as my mother's love was complemented by my knowledge that my father also deeply loved me, the love I feel from Melissa is complemented by the deep acceptance I feel from Michael.

It is not that I merit this love and acceptance. It seems to flow from all these human sources as an act of grace. I certainly don't believe that the experience of grace is unique to bisexuals. Much of the love I experience has nothing to do with sexuality or gender, such as the love I receive from friends, fellow church members, and clinical colleagues.

Yet there is a completeness of my experience of love, partly because I have received it from both a mother and a father, from both male and female siblings, and now from both a male and female lover. This sense of fullness of love from both genders is very special, and receiving both the feminine and the masculine expressions of love, love from persons of each gender, seems natural to me as a bisexual. It is a special gift to be able to give and to receive love – in all its forms – from both genders. To give and receive not just emotionally and spiritually but physically as well is a rich blessing.

CHAPTER 27
SEXUALITY REEXAMINED

One of the great benefits of my bisexual experience is that I have learned to continually question categories. For example, if a bisexual man is with a woman and finds her delicate features and her soft skin attractive, and these become eroticized, then what is to prevent his enjoying delicate features or soft skin in a man? Or if another man's toned muscular body is a turn-on, why can't the well-toned body of a woman be attractive? This spreading of erotic stimuli between the two genders isn't an automatic response in bisexuals. But bisexuals do have the experience of being aroused by two different sets of characteristics. It's an opportunity to question categories and assumptions.

Biracial people have a similar experience, as I've learned from our two children. I have heard their own views of racial dualism, the definition of people as white or non-white. Old laws in some southern states defined a person as "colored" even if only a small percentage of her or his ancestry was African. Society also polarizes gay and straight, and the stigma of being unnatural or weird falls on all who are not clearly and fully members of the dominant group. But those of us who don't fit neatly into these boxes of black OR white, gay OR straight, tend not to see the traditional boundaries as barriers. We may reinterpret rules that others take for granted.

For example, the concept of monogamy in the gay male subculture is different from in the heterosexual married definition. Gay men jokingly say that for gays, monogamy means "I have sex with my gay partner more than with anyone else!" But it's true that most gay male couples do not place a high value on traditional monogamy; what they care about is that their own union comes first. For most (not all) gay men, outside sex is not seen as threatening unless the third person intends to lure the partner away from his mate and break up the couple.

In the 1960s and 1970s some heterosexual couples experimented with a similar approach, called open marriage. Some continue today but they're in the minority, while for gay male couples open relationships are the norm. Perhaps open marriages fail with women because the woman has less power in the relationship and is more easily exploited. Perhaps they work for men because men tend to experience sex as fun, exciting, and not necessarily tied to a deep emotional commitment – or at least not tied to a commitment over a long period of time.

Thomas Moore, in his thoughtful book *Care of the Soul*, argues against recreational sex, stating that where soul meets body, it inevitably creates a bond between the two participants. There is a deep truth in Moore's observation that should not be treated lightly. Some men, in a casual sexual interaction, carefully avoid any prolonged eye-to-eye contact; I think this means that they hope to avoid soul meeting body in this relationship.

I have tried to think about the varieties of relationships I've had in which sex seemed appropriate – some of them deeply loving, some of them playful yet respectful, some of them lustful. Certainly Moore's image of soul meeting body applies to deeply loving sexual relationships. But what about non-sexual interactions that are playful? When Nick and I spontaneously skipped across Michigan Avenue, the joy and spontaneity seem to me to have been soulful. I can imagine having experiences like that with someone I hardly know, especially if we are in a workshop together where other emotional exchanges are deep, and silliness and humor follows such sharing.

Suppose after an afternoon in a workshop like that, two people gravitate to each other, perhaps go out for an evening meal together, and then end up in bed. Suppose they have no expectations of a relationship beyond the few days that they are in this particular city, attending this particular conference. Does that mean that when their souls meet their bodies in joy or pleasure or relief, the bond that is created is only valid if it involves commitment or some sense of permanence? Is the work of the Holy Spirit limited to situations that are planned, consciously decided, and rule-bound?

~ ~ ~

What is it that Moore is rejecting when he argues against recreational or casual sex? If he means that if there is to be sex between two persons, it should entail a willingness to see each other eye to eye and handle or acknowledge whatever emotions emerge in the immediate relationship, I agree. However, in a pickup situation, I would have different expectations. Say I meet another gay or bi man on the dance floor of a gay bar, and the other man begins touching me in ways that are clearly sexualized. If he suggested we spend the night together, it would be an open question as to whether he hopes we can meet, soul and body, or whether he is simply craving a sexual interaction. I would not agree to such an arrangement without realizing in my heart that it may turn out to involve some care of his soul. But I also would not assume that, if our bodies intertwine, we would necessarily touch one another's souls.

And what is wrong with pleasing another person sexually, even if there is no deep emotional relationship? Why do we support a morality of serious sex, and reject the appropriateness of playful sex? Assuming precautions are taken to avoid hurting anyone else involved, either physically or psychologically, why can't a sexual interaction be legitimate simply because it pleases both people?

I would add two caveats. Playful sex between two people may be ethical if there is enough respect between them that neither is exploiting the other, and if there is enough trust between them so each feels sure the other will not act in ways that risk pregnancy or transmission of sexual diseases. Non-exploitation includes respect of the other's reputation, which would preclude anyone's bragging or gossiping about the intimacies that he had enjoyed with the other.

When I began to accept my own bisexuality, my understanding of responsible sexual behavior expanded. At first I felt that homosexual experience was acceptable (given that I had been honest and worked out agreements with Melissa) because it met a need in myself that my wife could not meet. Since I had experienced attraction to men as well as to women, I could argue for non-monogamous relationships. Over time, in both my marriage and in my ongoing and deeply personal sexual friendships with other gay or bi men, I realized that having sex with a significant partner is not always a deep expression of love. Sometimes, even within a committed relationship, sex is simply a joyful, fun-filled release.

We have tended to assume that we must affirm either recreational sex or relationship sex: that if we recognize that sexual relationships may be powerful and deep, sex is only legitimate within a context of commitment.

Once, when I was engaged in a discussion of ethics with a university chaplain, he asked, "Why would you want sex that is like a short-order hamburger if you could have sex that is like a meal prepared by a chef who's an expert in your favorite cuisine?" I responded, "When I have time to relax and savor a really fine meal, then that is my preference. But if I'm on a long drive and simply want to alleviate my hunger, why should I refuse a hamburger?"

I think a better metaphor is music. When I had learned to enjoy the depth and power of classical music, no other form of music could satisfy me at the same level. A Brahms symphony moves me in a way that no piece of folk music can. But there are times when I have no need to reach that depth. At those times, I want to enjoy something light and pleasant, and a lovely ballad can meet that need.

~ ~ ~

In the context of rejecting the idea that heterosexuality is the only legitimate sexual experience, Perry Deane Young said, "All we are saying is that we exist, and nothing we do in private is as unnatural as forcing a person to live as a heterosexual when he knows he is not." I wonder if it is equally unnatural to force some people to live monogamously. Of course what is natural is not necessarily good. But usually when we go against nature, we do so at our own peril.

I am not arguing that monogamy is wrong; in some couples, both partners may feel that monogamy is a natural outgrowth of the love and commitment they feel toward each other. Such relationships do occur in nature; there are after all a few species of birds that do mate for life (although field studies show that these species are a small minority). But appealing to nature to defend heterosexual monogamy as the norm is only possible if you are uninformed about animal behavior, cross-cultural data on human sexuality, and the diversity of sexual behavior approved in different parts of the Christian Bible. [14]

It seems to me that there are some situations in which it is acceptable for a person to have sex with the partner of another person, if both of the committed partners have agreed. In most cases, this would mean they have agreed upon an open relationship. But it does not mean that it is open for both of them.

A few years ago I visited a gay male couple in another city. When I first arrived the three of us had a meal together and caught up on each other's lives. I have known Al for decades and was pleased to learn that he had been reading my most recent book, *Exploring the Spiritual*. Al said, " I especially liked that you realized not everyone wants to or is able to work out explicit agreements about open marriage, and that you weren't judgmental about that."

I knew that Al admired how Melissa and I have been able to discuss my bisexuality and reach agreements about non-monogamous sex. What followed both surprised and puzzled me.

I had sensed on previous visits that Hank, the younger of the two men, was interested in a sexual experience with me, but I had felt loyal to Al. After our meal, Al excused himself, saying he needed to go visit someone in the hospital. With his partner Hank sitting nearby, Al looked directly at me and stated, "I'll be gone for at least two hours".

Al seemed to be delivering a message which Hank understood. As soon as Al was out the door, Hank moved over to my chair, sat down on the floor in front of me, and said that he'd like to have sex with me. I gently pushed him away, saying "It's not that I wouldn't enjoy it – but I just don't know what it would mean to Al if he knew, and I don't want to hurt my friendship with him." Hank's response was, "You know, Dave, I don't think Al would really mind."

I asked him how he knew that. Hank smiled and said that he and Al had talked about it the last time I visited. He paused, as if he didn't want to reveal too much of what had been discussed. But then he said, "Well, Al simply said, 'Hank, I don't think we'll be having a three-way.'"

David R. Matteson

I understood. Al knew that Hank was interested in recreational sex with me and didn't think it would be a threat to their relationship, even though Al didn't want to join in. So he had given Hank a message that this would be a good time for Hank to pursue what he desired.

~ ~ ~

Suppose a man has shed the shackles of sexual inhibitions, has experienced sex with both men and women, and has learned to want sex for both Love and Joy. Won't he constantly be seeking satiation?

You might think so, if you are lost in your head. To live in one's body leads to moments of satiation and bliss, but also to a sense of being grounded. One does not always seek the perfect or the unlimited. One learns to enjoy the moment and to be deeply grateful for it.

My moments of quiet happiness are at their strongest after orgasm, in the wonderful peacefulness of feeling connected, almost one with another person. That peace often returns hours later, and although the excitement is diminished, the sense of oneness is still strong: oneness not just with a particular person, but with the whole of life, with the universe. The fun and joy of an unexpected and spontaneous act of sexual enjoyment cannot be compared with the beauty and depth of an act of union with someone I've known for years and deeply love. They are different experiences. But they are connected in one important sense. In both cases I feel gratitude. I thank the universe for its grace.

CHAPTER 28
YIELDING TO LIFE

At times I'm in situations where almost no one knows about my being bisexual. For example, in 2008 I attended a huge conference of psychologists because the publisher of my last book wanted me to be present for an authors' signing event. This involved my flying to Boston, the city where I had completed my doctorate exactly 40 years earlier, and where I had had my first homosexual dreams and fantasies. For me, the area was laden with homosexual longing. But most of the people with whom I was socializing – my publisher, the other authors with newly published books, and fellow psychologists – knew nothing of my bisexual identity. In most social settings, people generally assume a person is heterosexual until some direct information or subtle signal suggests otherwise. Therefore I had control of what cues I gave out about my life: I could discuss being married and raising children. Or having a gay lover. Or authoring a book on spirituality. Or my research on bisexuality.

In contrast, the year before the Boston trip I was with my lover Michael in Florida, in settings where most of the people were LBGT. When we saw two men walking together in the halls or the streets, we assumed that they were a gay couple.

In both Boston and Florida, I stayed in bed and breakfasts. Each morning I ate with a mixture of people, some of whom I had just met and some of whom I'd met a day or more before. And in both Boston and Florida, a part of me was closeted. In Boston people assumed I was straight until I said something about my lover Michael. In Florida people assumed I was gay until I mentioned my adult children or my wife.

Either way, there's always a decision to be made about coming out. Often it doesn't matter. I'm not uncomfortable with people making a wrong assumption if it's simply that they don't know all of me. However, if someone expresses something homophobic (which is all too common in the US), I sometimes surprise people by deliberately mentioning some male friend of mine and his male partner. Of course, the fact that I know someone who's gay doesn't mean I'm gay. But it makes it clear that we live among people of various sexual orientations, and thus it breaks the assumption that the current setting is an exclusively heterosexual one.

There is always the possibility of avoiding the issue and just enjoying being treated as "normal." And there are many times – usually when I do not expect to have continued contact with a person or group – that I do that.

However, research has shown that the most important reason people begin to overcome their homophobia is finding out that someone they already know and like is gay. Sometimes the purpose of my coming out is to break through a social assumption. But more often I hope for more: that people will begin to see that someone who shares some of their interests and values happens to be gay or bi, or knows LBGT people.

Being bisexual is only one facet of my personhood, and it helps for the other person to know some other facets first. If they've already gotten some sense of me as a person, they are less likely to reduce their view of me to a stereotype of whatever bi means to them. So in new social situations I talk about whatever others have brought up. I may let them know that I care passionately about the environment, or like to observe the family patterns of the swans in the park, or love the music of Mahler. I try to find some common ground.

David R. Matteson

In almost every conversation, people make assumptions. In some conversations I've joined, there's been an assumption that all of us present are liberals, and that means we are all going to vote for the Democratic or Green Party candidate. It can be helpful to gently question assumptions in order to nudge people to keep the discussion more open and risk actually being changed by it. If I can help to make the group a safe place for people to admit differences or disagreements, it's more likely that we can discuss homophobia in a more personal way – rather than in whatever way that social group sees as politically correct.

~ ~ ~

As I had learned years before, when I'm busy living both my married life and my gay life, it is important that I spend time alone, centering, being clear as to who I am and what I'm about.

After returning from India, I spent about two years trying to reach inward through practicing meditation using the classic cross-legged seated position in the Vipassana Buddhist tradition. I found that this approach doesn't help me get grounded or find inner stillness, so I decided to experiment with moving meditation. I began to learn T'ai Chi. It is a flowing and aesthetically beautiful practice, and when a number of people are moving together in synchrony, there is a sense of connectedness, similar to the experience of several people singing together in harmony. Each individual is doing his own thing, but all are in tune with the others. Although these aspects of T'ai Chi were very appealing to me, once again I found myself scrambling inside to do it right, distracted from just being in the now.

I decided to try a third approach to meditation: to be alone in silence, but to move by inventing my own choreography. This more spontaneous approach to movement makes use of my love of modern dance. It is not a performance, but an expression of my own inner feelings. This has proved to be the best form of meditation for me.

After a couple of years of using my own style of meditating, I went to a conference at which the American Buddhist leader Jack Kornfield taught lovingkindness meditation, and Stanislav Grof, a psychotherapist, used a type of highly expressive self-guided therapy.

The conference also featured a man who led classical sitting meditation twice each day. During a question-and-answer period, a woman in the audience asked, "Because I have a back problem, sitting meditation is very difficult for me physically. I want to do meditation lying down. Can you give me some tips?"

The trainer replied, "The classical sitting pose has thousands of years of use. It is the correct pose to use."

I could see the woman slump in disappointment as she took in his response. I remembered that in my suitcase back in the lodge I had some materials from my recent trip to India. Among them was a pamphlet on Buddhist meditation with sketches of several ancient meditation postures – one of them a reclining posture.

The next day I gave the pamphlet to the woman, saying with a wry smile, "I just want to be sure you understand what the classic postures are." I pointed to the lying down posture.

When she passed me on the path the following day, she greeted me joyfully, and thanked me profusely for affirming what she knew was right for her.

~ ~ ~

When my own back problems began in 2002, chronic pain was new to me. Previous physical hardships had only been a temporary interruption to my overall sense of wellbeing and health. But this time the back pain threatened to be permanent, and it began to limit my favorite activity, overseas travel.

My first priority was to figure out treatments that helped. After diagnosis by five different types of medical professionals, I needed to conduct my own experiments, one approach at a time, with different painkillers, exercises, supportive cushions, and so on. I kept careful records of the levels of pain I experienced with each, which helped me sort out what worked best for me.

When I had done all that I could to reduce the pain, I shifted to the inner work of learning to accept pain, rather than fight it. I found support by reading American Buddhist writings on suffering. [15] Paradoxically, after accepting at a fairly deep level that this pain might be a part of my daily experience for the rest of my life, I began to feel considerably better and was able to stop using pain medicines, except on days when I was making long flights or driving for hours.

Relinquishing unrealistic goals and letting go of control is a continuous process. Although the letting go actually seems to have helped, I can't unambiguously state that it was the cause of the decreased pain. There are no guarantees about the future, and although I have not needed regular medication for about eleven years, I must acknowledge the possibility that the pain may come back. But I have developed increased confidence in my ability to relax into pain, so I am less afraid of its return.

~ ~ ~

Sometimes the tendency to reach outward for validation, the need for social support, is appropriate. But sometimes it is dysfunctional. There are times when I simply need to do what is right for me and not worry about whether others understand.

Looking in the mirror when I shave in the morning, I sometimes catch myself carrying on a silent dialogue, trying to explain to someone about my bisexuality. Usually I'm arguing with a conservative Christian who sees gay sex as sinful, or a person with no understanding of minorities who sees equal rights as a threat. Perhaps most people can't understand my bisexuality – sometimes I don't understand it myself! Perhaps it just *is*, and needs no explanation or validation.

CHAPTER 29
SOUL FORCE

The experience was a quiet one; in fact, it mostly took place in silence. I was part of a group of people coming from many states and backgrounds; some of us had traveled many hours. We met in Indianapolis in 2004. The action was a vigil, standing silently in a line two blocks long on a sidewalk facing the city's convention center. The center was hosting the governing assembly of the Southern Baptist Convention, a denomination that was distributing to their youth a booklet arguing that God condemns sexually active gays, lesbians, and bisexuals.

The denomination had chosen to write *about us*, but they refused to speak directly *with us*: gay/lesbian/bisexual Christians and their allies. We were there to witness that "there should be no action about us without us," a basic guideline for maintaining respect put forth by the Brethren Mennonite Council in 2005.

SoulForce, the organization holding the vigil, was founded by ordained minister Mel White and his partner Gary Nixon. This nonviolent group opposed the Southern Baptists' spiritual violence against gays' natural orientation. The grandson of Mahatma Gandhi helped develop their approach, and the organization's name is a translation of *satyagraha,* the Sanskrit word Gandhi invented to describe his method. To participate in this vigil, each of us agreed to undergo training in nonviolence. We also agreed to a set of principles which included these statements:

1. My adversary is also a child of the Creator; we are both members of the same human family; we are sisters

and brothers in need of reconciliation.

2. My adversary is not my enemy but a victim of misinformation, as I have been.

3. My only task is to bring my adversary truth in love (through relentless but nonviolent action).

- SoulForce, 2005

Before each period of participation in the vigil, we had training sessions and a meditation period led by the Rev. James Larson, a Methodist minister who had helped Martin Luther King train demonstrators in non-violent methods.

As delegates to the Baptist convention passed us, we stood silently, handing them flyers explaining the reasons for our vigil.

Each time we saw someone about to walk by, we were to look that person in the eyes and ask ourselves silently, "Do I really believe this person is also a child of the Creator? Do I accept him/her as my brother/sister?"

Unless we felt that we were passing information to another child of the Creator, we were to look down, stand in silence, and instead of acting, focus inwardly on our own need for reconciliation. The intent was that we only speak the truth (as we know it) in love. We were not to interact in a way that expressed anger or treated the adversary as inferior. We are all sisters and brothers in need of reconciliation.

During the several days of the vigil, the meditation period created a sense of community, so when we were on the line and standing face-to-face with an adversary we did not stand alone but stood as part of that community.

Although I have participated in numerous rallies, vigils, and demonstrations, never have I felt so keenly that each encounter was not just an effort for justice but a prayer for my own humanity. In this way of being, there really is "soul force," a spiritual stance that transcends our own egos or opinions.

~ ~ ~

A number of themes have come together for me in recent years:
- There has been a gradual increase in my acceptance of my body, in contrast to my adolescent years and my struggle around athletics.
- I have felt a deep acceptance of who I am from those who know most aspects of my life, including my bisexuality – specifically from within my church, from my clinical support group, and from my closest friends.
- I have noted that my bisexual experience has reached a kind of loving stability, with both Melissa and Michael accepting the other's role in my life.

It is hard to describe the feelings related to these themes – they don't necessarily lend themselves to rational description. A shift in my attitude toward the Universe seems to be flowing from these experiences. This change is nowhere near complete, but at times I feel I have less of a "quarrel" with the Universe. It's as if my bisexual experience has helped me to respond to the suffering in the Universe in a way that is somewhat new to me.

Recently I woke up feeling a bit depressed and randomly opened a book on my nightstand, seeking guidance the way some people open a Bible in hope that God will show them a relevant verse. I found a poem by Rumi.

> Today...we wake up empty
> and frightened. Don't reach for the key
> to the study and begin reading.
> Take down the dulcimer.
>
> Let the beauty we love be what we do.

I Took Both Roads

> There are hundreds of ways
> to kneel and kiss the ground.
> - Jalál Ad-Din Muhammad Rumi
> (translated by Coleman Barks)

I mentioned to my wife how beautifully that poem captured how I feel on many mornings when I lie with unopened eyes, sensing the echoes of yesterday's news of war or the suffering of friends I visit in hospice. It isn't till I get out of bed, see the sunshine and the beautiful woods nearby, smell the lilacs or look at the wildflowers, that the beauty awakens the joy in me.

But today I woke up feeling joyful. "What is different?" I asked myself. It is not that I have avoided listening to the news, or that I haven't been in touch with those in pain. But two days ago I had sung some hymns in a community I treasure. I had spent some time playing with two of my grandchildren. I had met with a friend of thirty-some years. And I had talked with Melissa about some things that matter to us both.

The difference was that I was holding the joys and sorrows in a constant sense of relatedness. The highs and lows were set in the context of community. In addition, throughout the day there were periods of silence, times when I could catch my breath and deepen my roots. I felt connected, but also grounded.

CHAPTER 30
"AS GOOD AS IT GETS"

Sometime after Melissa's mother died in 2008 the two of us were discussing plans for our own deaths. Each of us had written down things we wanted included in our memorial services: portions of scripture, readings, hymns, and especially music that we might want played.

Melissa loves choral music and has borrowed more than one of my CDs by gay men's choruses to listen to in her car when driving alone. Sometime in 2009 Melissa came home from a trip by herself.

"I've been listening to the recording of 'Kumbaya' performed by Michael's Gay Men's Chorus," she said. "This arrangement is the most beautiful one I've heard. Will you please add it to the list of music I'd like for my memorial service?"

Of course I will honor Melissa's request. But I was also touched by the implication of this request. It suggests that she was picturing me present at her memorial service, grieving for her but listening to Michael's voice among those who were comforting me. So her memorial service was being conceived as a service honoring Melissa's life, but with Michael present in his singing.

To me, this confirms that Melissa trusts that Michael has no intention of diminishing the importance she has for me and will continue to honor her role in my life even after she dies. Surely this is testimony to a love that transcends ourselves and continues through others.

~ ~ ~

As I write this, more than 45 years since I first realized I was bisexual and more than 55 years since I felt the shaking of my theological foundations, I still feel grounded in love. Yet occasionally fear emerges. It comes from recognizing the implications of living out a radical love. By radical love I mean much more than the romantic love our culture idolizes; I mean the love that cares deeply about those who are different from oneself, love that is willing to maintain human respect even for one's enemies.

Recently I attended my denomination's national conference in Salt Lake City, one of the most conservative cities in our nation. As I toured the city, our guide, who appeared to be in his mid to late 20s, told us that he came from four generations of Mormons. My hunch was that he was gay.

The tour included a choice between two restaurants where we could eat lunch at no extra cost. Everyone else chose the first restaurant, but I deliberately asked the guide to show me the second one, which gave me a ten-minute walk in which to converse with him alone. When we had left the group behind, I told him "I am bisexual, and I wonder if you know anything about the gay bars in town? Is there one in which there will be other guys my age? One that's more of a neighborhood bar than a cruising bar."

He immediately told me "There are only two gay bars in town. One of them is a friendly neighborhood bar, but most of the patrons will be younger than you. I'll tell you where it is."

That evening, I went to the bar the guide suggested. I carried my glass of wine outside, where two men were sitting at a picnic table. I pulled up a chair nearby, waiting to see if they would provide an opening for me join them.

Eventually the men welcomed me into their conversation about what it's like to be gay in a mostly Mormon state. They asked me about my religious background, and I told them that I belong to a liberal denomination which has accepted les-bi-gays for decades.

David R. Matteson

The older man asked, "Are you by any chance attending the Unitarian Universalist convention in town?"

"Yes!, I responded, surprised that he knew about it.

"I read about it in the paper a few days ago. Welcome to Salt Lake City."

He continued to chat with the younger man and me for five or ten minutes and then left. The younger man turned to me. "I'm on a spiritual quest myself. I'd like to know more about you and your religion."

It was clear early in our encounter that neither of us was seeking a sexual relationship, and all it took was my genuine curiosity about his spiritual search to move the conversation to a deeper level. We continued to talk for at least an hour, one of those amazingly personal conversations that sometimes occur with someone you'll probably never see again. Finally I stood up and said I had to leave. His immediate response was "Thank you for listening. This has been the most valuable conversation I've had in over a year."

Of course it would have been harder for me to have provided the space for such a conversation if I didn't have both Michael and Melissa in my life. The fact that I have two wonderfully loving and satisfying relationships leaves me with inner space just to be with a young man who longed for permission to explore. It also allowed me to genuinely accept his exploration, because I have taken the risks to find my own "road less traveled" – in fact, to take both roads.

My sexuality is not the only area in which I have taken both paths. So many times, instead of deciding between two contrasting elements, I have enjoyed exploring both and affirming both. By the time I reached my sixties, I had chosen both paths in a number of life areas:

After receiving my doctorate, I chose to pursue both **counseling and teaching** and sought a university position in which my time was fairly evenly divided between the psychology department and the University counseling service.

Throughout my career I was both a practicing therapist (as a counselor, a mental health worker, and in private practice) and a scientific researcher, combining **humanistic practice** with **scientific research**. I was trained both in **theology** and in **psychology** and continued an interest in both **empirical science** and **spirituality**. My epistemology embraced both science (for the observable world), and mysticism (for the personal, experiential domain and spirituality).

My embrace of the **women's movement** blended with my involvement in the **men's movement**. I was interested in both the pro-feminist political view (men's feminism, NOMAS, and the Men and Masculinity conferences), and the mythopoetic and artistic aspects of the new men's movement (led by Robert Bly).

I am very grateful to live in one of the most diverse multi-ethnic cultures on earth, the United States of America. Yet I love living in and attempting to understand other cultures. I cherish both the **freedom of the West** and the **connectedness of the East**.

With my wife Melissa, I've helped create an **interracial family** which includes black, white, and bi-racial Americans and an extended family that includes grandchildren of European, Asian, African, and Native American descent.

I have extensive experience as a **counselor** but also as a **client**. The repercussions of my father's death led to my choosing to enter therapy with **two different therapists simultaneously**: a man and a woman.

Finally, I have lived in both the **heterosexual and homosexual subcultures** and had **both male and female partners**. I am in a deeply committed primary relationship with Melissa, but I also have a gay lover who is a regular travel partner and with whom I spend time both at his home and at my own.

I hate choices that imply exclusivity. Much of life is NOT a zero-sum game; when you win on one side, you do not necessarily lose on the other. When you affirm your need to be alone at times (introversion), that may actually increase your ability to be genuinely present with other people, to be extraverted, at other times. When you love men, it doesn't necessarily mean you don't love women.

~ ~ ~

In recent months, Melissa and I have spent a lot of time together exploring places that we might live in the next phase of our lives. We are getting too old to climb on roofs, rake leaves, or empty gutters. We need a more elder-friendly space.

Our task involves seeing accurately what is available for "senior living" and assertively asking questions. We are trying to find a place nearly as beautiful as the scenes from the windows and decks of our current home, which overlooks a small ravine and looks toward a descending stream complete with mallard ducks and a pair of great blue herons. As I write these words, I'm sitting in my favorite study – the screen house behind our home. Lush woods embrace me on three sides. It is so wonderfully quiet and peaceful, tucked into the woods at the end of a semi-rural dead end street.

I wish life could be so good for everyone. The conference I just attended was heavy on social responsibility and justice. I will continue to work for peace, for equality, and for justice. I'm acutely aware that some of the peace I have in this beautiful setting comes from white male privilege. I also know the best way to work for peace is to come from a place of peace deep in our hearts. I try to keep my body open to joy and my heart open to love. World peace is more likely to emerge when we accept ourselves, when we feel radically accepted by a community of love and by the universe itself.

The path of my life has moved to greater and greater openness, first at the church, then at the university. Now I am performing the boldest coming out of my life – putting my story in print, using my real name, and using the word bisexual in the title. Of course I have no way of predicting who might see the book on the shelf of a bookstore or online and read my name as author. Nor will I be able to control whom they gossip to about what they have seen.

Now we are considering moving to a religiously oriented retirement community. About once a week, as I am awakening, I fantasize that our neighbors there are gossiping. "Did you know Dave Matteson is bisexual? Why do you suppose Melissa puts up with it? Can we allow that in a Christian retirement community?"

Melissa gives me a warm hug and assures me, "After 53 years of loving each other, the neighbors aren't going to separate us."

At the beginning of this book, I told about the dream that first signaled to me that I was bisexual. Recently, I had another vivid dream. I took it to mean that the Muse was suggesting I end this memoir as I began it. So here is the second dream:

It is a pleasant, sunny day, and I'm sitting outdoors on a grassy bank. There are hundreds of people around me: a large crowd meeting in silence, as if it's a vigil or some occasion for reverence. There's a nun standing in front of me – at least I think she's a nun. She's close to 50 in age, wearing a beautiful garment made of a beige fabric similar to the homespun cotton Gandhi wove. From a graceful hood that loosely covers her head, the fabric flows down over her body and almost to the ground; it reveals the graceful curved female shape of her body in a natural way, quite unlike the way the habits of most religious orders try to hide a nun's body. It is somewhat like an Indian woman's sari, but more subtle, with less fabric and quietly sensual. The total impression is like a modern wood sculpture, slightly abstract with every curve and line being soft, simple, and elongated.

I contemplate whispering to her, "I think your clothes are beautiful."

There is a long silence.

I'm conscious that if she's a nun, it's likely she is not used to being admired or complimented for her looks. I do not see her as sexual. I am afraid she will misunderstand my complement as a come-on. I speak to her, but my spontaneous words sound clumsy: "I think your clothes are very sensible."

I immediately feel that the words do not express what I meant to communicate. I wake up, feeling disappointed.

Sometimes we communicate in ways that play it safe. I want to be accepted; perhaps I'm still overly "rejection-sensitive," as one of my therapists put it decades ago. The rejection I felt or imagined in adolescence may still distort my communications, despite the fact that I'm now outgoing and gregarious.

I believe the series of dreams I've had in the last couple of weeks have to do with the process of writing this memoir. I have fears that people who have up till now viewed me as warm and interesting and caring will read about my life and be shocked at how much I have been willing to communicate through sexual experiences, and how valuable these experiences have been to me.

The great myth collector Joseph Campbell, who argued for the commonality of mythology across cultures, was often quoted as advising youth, "Follow your bliss." At first I misunderstood his phrase to mean *pursue the pleasures and experiences which make you happy.* But I now think the phrase is much more grounded than that. I now interpret it as *do what you authentically long to do, so that your acts convey your deeper truth.*

This means speaking honestly from the heart: not hurtfully, but honestly. In my dream of the nun, I am afraid of her reactions. I fail to ground myself in my own perceptions and share my own feelings; thus I miss an opportunity to get to know her. Communication is like breathing – every breath out needs to be followed by a breath in. But if I exhale a compromised and dulled expression of my authentic self, such as "I think your clothes are sensible", any response I receive back is likely to be confused rather than revelatory of the other person. The nun doesn't know who I really am, and I am unlikely to get to know who she is.

My calling is to speak my truth in love, and to listen to the other's truth. In the dream, I speak not out of love but out of fear. Too often that is the case in many of our lives. We fear showing our true selves.

~ ~ ~

My hope is that Melissa and Michael and I will have another decade to continue our ministries. Michael, as an archeologist and scholar of the Old Testament, has a wonderfully rich store of knowledge with which to help people in Christian churches rethink their fear and hatred of homosexuality. Melissa, as a nurse administrator, has a passion for work in Africa, supporting innovative projects that help HIV-positive orphan children. My own special ministry is to les-bi-gays, especially other bisexuals and their partners. If the sharing of my life story gives you some better understanding and deeper acceptance of others who are bisexual, as well as a sense of hope that you can dare to find and follow *your* unique path, I will be grateful.

I began with a poem and will end with one.

David R. Matteson

THE ANDROGYNE

for I am as much
the dark
as I am the light
these letters
on paper
the afternoon
shadows
the black matrix
of stars

to give up the one
is to diminish
the other
for I am as much the silence
as I am the sound

I stand
on the balancing beam
in the eye
of the storm
making love

for love
alone.

> \- Franklin Abbott
> *Mortal Love: Selected Poems* 1971-1998

Thank you for reading.
Please review this book. Reviews help others find Absolutely Amazing eBooks and inspire us to keep providing these marvelous tales.

If you would like to be put on our email list to receive updates on new releases, contests, and promotions, please go to AbsolutelyAmazingEbooks.com and sign up.

About the Author

David Matteson taught psychology and counseling for almost three decades at Governor's State University, south of Chicago, an educational institution founded on experiential teaching. He holds an undergraduate degree in psychology from Alfred University, a graduate degree in theology from Colgate Rochester Crozer Divinity School, and a Ph.D. in counseling from Boston University. He has been a practitioner both in the ministry and in secular mental health. Dr. Matteson helped found a psychology department at Marietta College in Ohio, and later was Director of Mental Health Services in Washington County Ohio.

His published works include chapters in several books, research in such journals as *Adolescence, American Psychologist, Developmental Psychology, The Family Psychologist, Individual Psychology, Journal of Homosexuality,* and *Journal of Sex Research,* and has authored or co-authored two previous books, *Adolescence Today: Sex Roles and the Search for Identity,* and *Ego Identity: A Handbook for Psychosocial Research* (with James Marcia, Alan Waterman, et al.).

Matteson has lived in three very different cultures: American, Danish, and Indian, and has done research and taught graduate courses in all three.

REFERENCES

Abbott, Franklin. 1999. *Mortal Love: Selected Poems 1971-1998*. Liberty, TN: RFD Press.

Abernathy, Ralph David. 1989. *And the Walls Came Tumbling Down: An Autobiography*. New York: Harper and Row.

Adler, Alfred. 1917. *Study of Organ Inferiority and its Psychical Compensation*. Translated by S. E. Joliffe. New York: Nervous and Mental Disease Publishing Co.

Adler, Alfred. 1931. *What Life Should Mean to You*. Boston: Little, Brown and Company.

Bagemihl, Bruce. 1999. *Biological Exuberance: Animal Homosexuality and Natural Diversity*. New York: St. Martin's Press.

Barrington, Judith. 2000. *Lifesaving: A Memoir*. Portland, Oregon: The Eight Mountain Press.

Bergling, Tim. 2001. *Sissyphobia: Gay Men and Effeminate Behavior*. Portland, OR: Book News, Inc. distributed by Synetic Solutions, LLC.

Berne, Eric. 1964. *Games People Play*. Jackson, TN: Grove Press.

Bly, Robert. 1990. *Iron John: A Book About Men*. Reading, MA: Addison-Wesley.

Boswell, John. 1994. *Same-sex Unions in Pre-Modern Europe*. New York: Villard.

Elkins, David N. 1998. *Beyond Religion: A Personal Program For Building A Spiritual Life Outside The Walls Of Traditional Religion*. Wheaton, IL: Theosophical Publishing House.

Freeman, Lawrence. 2001. *Jesus: The Teacher Within*. New York: Continuum International Publishing Group.

Friedan, Betty. 1964. *The Feminine Mystique*. New York: Dell.

Glaser, Chris. 1988. *Uncommon Calling: A Gay*

Christian's Struggle to Serve the Church. San Francisco: Harper and Row.

Golding, William. 1954. *Lord of the Flies*. Boston: Fader & Fader.

Green, Richard. 1987. *The "Sissy Boy Syndrome" and the Development of Homosexuality*. New Haven: Yale University Press.

Hutchins, Loraine, and Kaahumanu, Lani, editors. 1991. *Bi Any Other Name: Bisexual People Speak Out*. Boston: Alyson Publications, Inc.

Kimmell, Michael S., and Messner, Michael A. 2001. *Men's Lives*, fifth edition. Boston: Allyn and Bacon.

Kohn, Barry, and Matusow, Alice. 1980. *Barry and Alice: Portrait of a Bisexual Marriage*. Englewood Cliffs, NJ: Prentice Hall.

Kopay, Dave, and Young, Perry Deane. 1980. *The David Kopay Story: An Extraordinary Self-Revelation*. New York: Arbor House.

LeVant, Ronald F., and Pollack, W. S. 1995. *New Psychology of Men*. New York: Basic Books.

Louganis, Greg, and Marcus, Eric. 1997. *Breaking the Surface: The Greg Louganis Story*. Naperville, IL: Sourcebooks.

Matteson, David R. 1974. "Changes in Attitudes Toward Authority Figures with the Move to College: Three Experiments." *Developmental Psychology*, 10, 3.

Matteson, David R. 1975. *Adolescence Today: Sex Roles and the Search for Identity*. Homewood, IL: Dorsey-Irwin Press.

Matteson, David R. 1977. " Exploration and Commitment: Sex differences and Methodological Problems in the Use of the Identity Status Categories." *Journal of Youth and Adolescence*, 6, 353-379.

Matteson, David R. 1977. "Stereotypes of Gay Men." Unpublished lecture delivered to Alternative Lifestyles seminar, Governors State University, University Park, Illinois.

Matteson, David R. 1985. "Bisexual Men in Marriages: Is a Positive Homosexual Identity and Stable Marriage Possible?" *Journal of Homosexuality*, 11, 149-173. Also reprinted in Klein, Fritz, and Wolf, Timothy J., editors. 1985. *Bisexualities: Theory and Research*. New York: Haworth Press.

Matteson, David R. 1991. "Attempting to Change Sex Role Attitudes In Adolescents: Explorations of Reverse Effects." *Adolescence*, 26, (104), 885-898.

Matteson, David R. 1993. "Differences within and Between Genders: A Challenge to the Theory." In *Ego Identity: A Handbook for Psychosocial Research*, edited by J. E. Marcia, A.S. Waterman, S.L. Archer, and J.L. Orlofsky, 69-110. New York: Springer-Verlag.

Matteson, David R. 1997. "Bisexual and Homosexual Behavior and HIV Risk Among Chinese-, Filipino-, and Korean-American Men." *Journal of Sex Research*, 34 (1), 93-104.

Matteson, David R. 1998. "Is Modernity Possible without Alienation? Marriage Choices of Indian and Indian-American Women." Unpublished manuscript.

Matteson, David R. 2008. *Exploring the Spiritual: Paths for Counselors and Psychotherapists*. New York: Taylor and Francis.

Nimmons, David. 2002. *The Soul Beneath the Skin: The Unseen Hearts and Habits of Gay Men*. New York: St. Martin's Press.

O'Neill, Nena, and O'Neill, George. 1972. *Open Marriage: A New Life Style for Couples*. New York: M. Evans & Company

Pleck, Joseph H. 1981. *The Myth of Masculinity*. Cambridge, MA: M.I.T. Press.

Redl, Fritz, and Wineman, David. 1951. *Children Who

Hate: A Sensitive Analysis of the Anti-Social Behavior of Children in their Response to the Adult World. New York: Free Press.

Roskelley, John. 1987. *Nanda Devi: The Tragic Expedition.* Seattle, WA: Mountaineers Books.

Schweitzer, Albert. 1905. *The Quest for the Historical Jesus: a Critical Study of its Progress from Reimarus to Wrede.* New York: Macmillan Co., 1964 [c1910].

Skoglund, J. E. & Matteson, D.R. 1961. "Making Dialogue Preach." *The Pulpit: A Journal of Contemporary Preaching,* August, vol. 32, no. 8, and pp. 8 – 9. Chicago.

Tillich, Paul. 1948. *The Shaking of the Foundations.* New York: Charles Scribner's Sons.

ENDNOTES

[1] "Fault Line," from Noisy Stones: A Meditation Manual, Skinner House Books, 1992. Permission granted by author.

[2] "You Are Accepted" is printed in the book *The Shaking of the Foundations* (Tillich, 1948).

[3] The United Methodist Church still has not affirmed either as of its 2012 national meetings. United Church of Christ affirmed inclusiveness of les-bi-gays in 1985. Unitarian Universalism (UU) has affirmed inclusiveness of sexual minorities since 1970; its affirmation of all religions goes back at least to the to the merger of Unitarian and Universalists in 1961. The first ordained clergy of any religion in the US or Canada to come out as gay was the UU Minister James Stoll in 1969.

[4] The move away from home was a key variable in my doctoral thesis. See Matteson, 1968, in references.

[5] The men's movement emerged in the 1980s, a quarter century after the renewal of the feminist women's movement that was most visibly initiated by Betty Friedan's book *The Feminine Mystique*. The men's movement was divided into three main groups: the pro-feminist, the anti-feminist, and the mythopoetic – this last led by Robert Bly. Bly conducted conferences and workshops for decades. Like the pro-feminist group, Bly's movement promoted men's owning and expressing their tender feelings. Bly also stressed the need for courage and taking action. In some senses, he advocated a type of androgyny: a melding of the positive traits of both masculinity and femininity.

[6] David N. Elkins, *Beyond Religion: A Personal Program for Building a Spiritual Life Outside the Walls of Traditional Religion,* 1998 pp.108-109.

[7] Over time I recognized that absent fathers have been the norm in most American families ever since the industrial revolution, when men's daily

work was no longer close to home. In the days when most fathers were farming, they worked on the same property where the children were raised. The effects of father absence became a major theme in my first book (*Adolescent Today: Sex Roles and the Search for Identity*, 1975).

[8] Raids certainly were part of gay history and were, in fact, the trigger for the 1969 riots that began the "Gay Liberation" movement in the US (when police raided the Stonewall bar in Greenwich Village in New York City).

[9] The major collection of writings on bisexuality wasn't published until 1991 (by Loraine Hutchins and Lani Kaahumanu). The Kinsey report on males had been published in 1948 but received mostly negative reporting on its data indicating the rates of homosexuality and the fact that a large percent of the sample were bisexual in behavior. In Chicago, the major gay/lesbian organization at that time, Horizons, did not add "bisexual" to its name until about 1985 (personal correspondence from Jim Klein, 2013).

[10] John Boswell, a prominent scholar of medieval Catholicism, discovered hidden away in the Vatican library the liturgies of 4th century commitment ceremonies for male couples. See Boswell, 1994, and Matteson, 2008, pp. 213-214.

[11] I appeared on these television shows in 1979 or 1980.

[12] The University continues to follow its original objectives:
"To study the mind of man in its realization of different aspects of truth from diverse points of view.
To bring into more intimate relation with one another, through patient study and research, the different cultures of the East on the basis of their underlying unity.
To approach the West from the standpoint of such a unity of the life and thought of Asia.
To seek to realize, in a common fellowship of study, the meeting of the East and the West, and thus ultimately to strengthen the fundamental conditions of world peace through the establishment of free communication of ideas between the two hemispheres."

[13] Jesus sometimes directly quotes the laws from Hebrew scripture, and disagrees with them. For example, "You have heard that it was said, 'an eye for an eye, and a tooth for a tooth', but I say unto you, 'Love your neighbor.

Be kind to those who persecute you.' " (Matthew 6:38-39, citing Exodus 21:24)

[14] See Jennifer Knust's scholarly yet fascinating book *Unprotected Texts: The Bible's Surprising Contradictions about Sex and Desire.*

[15] I especially recommend Tara Brach's *Radical Acceptance* (Bantam, 2003), Pema Chodron's *When Things Fall Apart* (1997, Shambhala), and Darlene Cohen's *Finding a Joyful Life in the Heart of Pain* (Shambhala, 2000).

The New Atlantian Library

NewAtlantianLibrary.com

or AbsolutelyAmazingEbooks.com

or AA-eBooks.com

www.ingramcontent.com/pod-product-compliance
Lightning Source LLC
Chambersburg PA
CBHW070728160426
43192CB00009B/1354